EDGE T

POETRY BY PETER DALE

Walk from the House
The Storms
Mortal Fire
Mortal Fire: Selected Poems
Cross Channel
One Another
Too Much of Water
A Set of Darts: Epigrams
(with W.S. Milne and Robert Richardson)
Earth Light

IN TRANSLATION

François Villon: Selected Poems
The Seasons of Cankam
(Translations from the Classical Tamil,
with Kokilam Subbiah)
Narrow Straits
Poems of Jules Laforgue
The Divine Comedy

Peter Dale

EDGE TO EDGE

NEW AND SELECTED POEMS

ANVIL PRESS POETRY

Published in 1996
by Anvil Press Poetry Ltd
69 King George Street London SE10 8PX

Copyright © Peter Dale 1996
Foreword copyright © Grey Gowrie 1996

ISBN 0 85646 272 1

A catalogue record for this book
is available from the British Library

Peter Dale has asserted his right under the Copyright, Designs and
Patents Act, 1988 to be identified as the author of this book

All rights reserved

This book is published with financial assistance from
The Arts Council of England

Designed and composed in Monotype Ehrhardt by
Anvil Press Poetry Ltd
Printed and bound in England by
The Alden Press, Oxford

FOR
WILLIAM COOKSON

ACKNOWLEDGEMENTS

I am grateful to the editors of the following publications in which versions of poems in the New Poems section first appeared: *Agenda*; *The Agenda Anthology* (Carcanet); *Completing the Picture* (Stride): *Le Journal des Poètes* (Brussels); *PN Review*; *The Zimbabwean Review*.

I would like to express my appreciation to the publishers of the following volumes for their help and support for this selection: *Mortal Fire: Selected Poems*; *One Another*; *Too Much of Water* – Agenda Editions. *Cross Channel*; *Earth Light* – Hippopotamus Press.

CONTENTS

Acknowledgements	VI
Foreword by Grey Gowrie	XIII
Author's Note	XV

from THE STORMS (1968)

Dedication	18
The Storms	19
Overnight Coach	21
Eighth Period	21
Single Ticket	23
Not Drinking Water	24
Last Respects	25
Meditation Down the Wards	25
Passing the Gates	26
Patient in a Ward	26
The Visitors	27
Just Visiting	28
Obtainable from All Good Herbalists'	29
from THE MONTHS	
Winter	30
Thrush	31
River-Garden	31
Bats	33

from MORTAL FIRE (1976)

Dedication	36
Walk from the House	37
Unaddressed Letter	37
The Fragments	38
Radium Therapy	41
from HAVING NO ALTERNATIVE	
Meeting	42
Courtesy Visit	43

The Terms	43
Thinking of Writing a Letter	44
Separation	46
Lullaby	46
Steps	46
Starting Your Travels	47
Damages	47
Full Circle	48
Thirty Summers	50
Terrace	50
Crowd	50
Old Poet on a Rainy Day	51

THE GOING

Wait and See	52
Tangibles	52
Country Walk	53
The Swifts	53
Silver Birch	54
Presence	54
Returns	55
Dusk	55
Gift of Words	55
Crocus	56
Sleep	57
Lullaby	57
Hold	57
Lost and Found	58
Old Haunt	58
Two Sparrows	59
Gifts	59
Meander	60
Keeper	60
Retrospect	60
Tie	61
Truce	61
Twilight	61
Deadlock	62
Impasse	62
Retraction	62
Insight	63

Keepsake	63
The Mind's Eye	64
Eidetic Image	65
Obsession	65
Vigil	66
Wild Flower	66

from CROSS CHANNEL (1977)

Recognition	71
Rain	71
Unspoken	72

ONE ANOTHER (1978)

FOREWORD	73
The Lane	74
Landscape	74
Dissolve	75
Response	75
Cone	76
Dialogue and Soliloquy	76
A Little Light	77
The Rose	77
Insights	78
Record	78
Talisman	79
Match	79
Silence	80
Declination	80
Aubade	81
Shadow	81
View	82
Music	82
Her Concentration on a Nutshell	83
Pressed	83
Sunset and Storm	84
Deed of Gift	84
Shades	85
Moon	85
Frost	86

Hand and Head	86
The Shadow	87
A Long Shot	87
The Thunder Stone	88
Storm	88
Walk	89
Bird's Eye	89
Memento	90
One Another	90
Dream	91
Compact	91
Comfort	92
Present	92
Inklings	93
Fledgling	93
Glimpses	94
Her Prophecy	94
Hearing the Flowers	95
Duotone	96
Spectrum	97
Clear Stream	97
Moth-Light	98
Dusk	98
The Game	99
Autumnal	99
The Oak	100
Before Sleep	100
Revenant	101
Clearing	101
Moth	102
Long Evenings	102
One Off	103
Memorial	103
Earth-bound	104
Window	104

from TOO MUCH OF WATER (1983)

Dedication	106
Last Wishes	107
Last Words	107

Spring	108
Interflora	108
Byway	108
Rendezvous	109
Word	110
Clusters	110
Moment	110
The Brooch	110
Path	112
Wall	112
Exorcism	113
Gifts	113
Against Superstition	114
Winters	114
Birds	115
An Apology	115
Summer Shadows	116

from EARTH LIGHT (1991)

Portents	121
Cranesbill	121
Gifts	122
Occasions	122
Willow Walk	123
Memento	123
Violets	124
Antique	124
Goldenrod	125
Bric-a-Brac	126
Mirrors	127
LIKE A VOW	
Local Colour	128
Recapitulation	128
Upland	130
The Sunken Path	133
Gesture	135
The Hill	137
River	138
The Water-Splash	140

Still	141
Sun	142
Correspondences	142
Communication	143
Souvenir	143
Life-Lines	144
The Lost Ones	144
Steps	145
A Woman Speaks to God the Father	145
Homage to Robinson Jeffers	146
Memorial	147

MIRRORS, WINDOWS

A Likeness Reflects	148
The Garden Beyond	148
Reflection Answers Back	149
Reflection Rebukes and Challenges	150
The Garden Beyond and Beyond	150
Wise and Cautious	151
Reflection Heckles	152
Colloquy	152
He Addresses Himself to Reflection	153
Ventriloquy	154

NEW POEMS

A Time to Speak	157
Outcry	157
Platonic	158
Parting Gift	158
World Tour	159
Journey	159
Autumn Colour	160
Monologue	161
Bequest	162

Notes	165
Index of Titles	169

FOREWORD

There is a phrase by the American poet William Carlos Williams which makes me think of Peter Dale, a writer far removed from Williams in style and sensibility. It occurs in a curious (for Williams) poem about a lion ravishing a woman in the snow: 'a chastity packed with lewdness.' A puritan strain in English Literature, from Herbert to Milton, Bunyan to Blake, often delivers more in the way of sensuousness than poems allowed to wander where they will. You get the feeling of forms almost bursting under the pressure of the emotions they contain; read, in this selection, 'A Woman Speaks to God the Father', or, from a recent poem, 'Monologue':

> Years? It seems an aeon
> that I have kept faith,
> whatever that may mean
> without volition or oath.
> You left me little option –
> Your talents, your serial spleens!
> Always the exception,
> you with your fine lines.
>
> But I know what it means
> in slither, self-disgust,
> and icy blue moons.
> Not that you'd have guessed.
> Fat chance you're flesh and blood.
> The last far pane of light
> has flicked down like a lid.
> The night is absolute.

The idiom, the tone of voice is wholly of our time. The beat of the poem, which is where the emotion is stored, looks back to the great colloquial mainstream before specialized literary knowledge, in the neo-classical period, got at it. 'Who would true valour see, / Let him come hither; / One here will constant be, / Come wind, come weather.' Dale's poetry is non-conformist, sincere. It deals with the permanent things, love and death, but it wrestles to render them true as if the writer were suspicious of, as well as attracted by, the infinite stored seductions of our language.

Yet this poet can submit, with seeming ease, a masterly sonnet, 'Silence', which opens 'Clouds stilted along on two great spokes of light', phrases of Larkinesque memorability such as 'the living need a little love to go on' and lines like 'my love, you make the darkness personal.' Memorability needs more than sincerity, it needs wit. His imagery is unfashionably pastoral, in the love poems perhaps too much so, but there is a twentieth-century texture and verisimilitude in the schoolteaching ('All day I teach the children how thoughts are phrased') and hospital poems. Some of the latter have the intense concentration of Rembrandt etchings; they seem dark and conventional until you start to examine them properly.

Except for his Villon versions (not given here), which stand among the great modern translations, Peter Dale has been neglected in reputation. I hope this book will start to change things. He is the long-distance runner of his generation and it is exciting to follow his development. The governing characteristic of Dale's poetry is authenticity. His lines ring true because that is precisely what they are.

GREY GOWRIE

AUTHOR'S NOTE

This selection is made forward from *Mortal Fire: Selected Poems* (Agenda Editions/University of Ohio Press, 1976). Ironically, the grandiose but spurious sequence 'Mortal Fire' has been redistributed to show which poems were originally published in my first volume *The Storms* (Macmillan, 1968). 'The Going', from *Mortal Fire: Selected Poems*, 1976, except for two poems, is intact; *One Another* (Carcanet/Agenda Editions, 1978) has lost three sonnets and gained one.

A selected should contain only the best poems, but such a book would have been depressingly and expensively slim. Since it is the failure to have judged previous books correctly that necessitates such a volume, it would be unwise to imagine that now one can ever get it right. Hindsight brings just another kind of partial judgement.

On the other hand, a selected is an author's last chance, perhaps, to set things straight. In looking over my early verse I have borne in mind Andrea del Sarto's point, though made in a somewhat different context; as Browning has it:

> That arm is wrongly put ...
>   ... and I could alter it:
> But all the play, the insight and the stretch –
> Out of me, out of me.

Nevertheless, a few silent changes to pointing and phrasing have been risked, a few excisions, a few telescopings. I can only hope that most of these are revisions and not revisionist.

PETER DALE

from THE STORMS

DEDICATION

*<u>H</u>ere, Ian, a few poems, <u>a</u> decade's debris,
<u>m</u>ade and emended <u>i</u>n odd moments.
<u>L</u>ines I like first <u>t</u>o leave with you
<u>o</u>nly, my friend. <u>N</u>ow free to all.*

The Storms

Losing my patience, setting type in the press
you gave me, I can hear your voice insist
Paul was no artist since he would untwist
knots you'd snip and slash. Such pithiness
from you, thought worthy once to break a spell
of silence, startles me and I recall
how far away you are, crowding with all
your work into a room in Camberwell.

Once, as I walked with your usual silent self,
you spoke out: A bag of peanuts equals the weight
of Boehme's works; your pockets bulged with great
wisdom but meagre food.
                         Here, on the shelf,
your Boehme lies. Thumbprints of paint edge
your favourite lines. They mark my books you read,
snatched in frenzy to back something you said,
or rammed beneath your easel as a wedge.

Outside the study window now the tree
I tried describing, you to draw, is a flare
of shuffling leaves. All that's left of the bare
boughs are my words and these two or three
sketches recalling how your hands would form
a winter-struck tree whenever you discussed
the way you start a carving. A slight gust
rustles the leaves but ushers in no storm.

Rainbow's trajectory zooms over the scarp
shoulder plunging straight into the town
huddled beneath the shelter of the down.
And I think of other trajectories: your sharp
erratic course through towns; sketches that lie
discarded in lodgings like a paper trail
no one can track; this tree you traced as a frail
skeletal hand to close against the sky.

The leaves will motley soon, ready to drop.
The first winds will flail the branches bare.
I set alight the sketches I kept; they flare,
darken and gnarl.... You could come and stop
the winter. Then perhaps your hands would rouse
to shape this tree again. The slate light
wouldn't disturb your photophobic sight.
Come and bring your storm into my house.

The window casts a broken shaft of light
towards the darkness. The valley lights wink out,
one at a time. Your tree rustles about
my shadowed head. This lamp is seen for quite
a distance. But not by you. Nothing can find
you in that darkness where your sketches sail
like papers from a house ransacked by gale.
Come back, for the storm beats into my mind.

I stare my face out, glad that some have sworn
we're brothers. But your nose is longer; your lips
curve with the sensuous line of women's hips –
mine are a scar. And brothers, I know, are born
of one woman's suffering. Yet I have led
your wandering life with you, and I have known
your hands gnarl into a tree of bone.
And, tonight, your storm beats into my head.

Last light vanishes. Cold night air creeps
under the doors and windows, up my back.
Wind begins to rush and with a crack
the branches sway. A single leave sweeps
against the pane, a moth the glass deceives.
Rain beats like canvas tearing. I draw
the blinds across the distorted face I saw.
Take shelter. Late birds bicker in the eaves.

Overnight Coach

Shot with sleep, the head slumps on the chest.
Ribs jolt against me every corner swing.

But I don't know your name or anything,
though my shoulder would afford some kind of rest.

I sit in arm's reach to cushion your back
but you have to lean against a travel bag.

And yet I stay awake in case you sag,
for then my hand could save your head a crack.

I watch the branches tearing great rents
across your face, projected as if dead.

And if I cannot shoulder your sleeping head
it is because time comes I may not raise

your bowed head from its tears. The road strays
briefly through England. And there are continents.

Eighth Period

Last year's sex-kitten, out of work again,
(mean effrontress, chased and bare)
saunters about the grounds with her great Dane,
as sandy blonde as that lassitude of hair –
boy-hunting, leash seductively in hand.
Four o'clock and time to make a stand.

I plot my progress through the room to reach
the window for a glimpse of her, compare
her insinuity with these hulks I teach,
mobile jumble sales with sweep's-brush hair.
One week to go. Difficult to think
by then they'll learn to dress like her and slink.

Drama for Today. She reads a speech,
a mother deprived of husband and only son
in the World War. (Once more undo her breach,
dear friends.) The long day's task is done.
The slumping class as usual does not hear,
luckily. She speaks with passion. And they'd jeer.

Only I hear and follow closely now,
head in the book to hide my smarting eyes,
tensing for fear I have to pick a row
with some lout there before that passion dies.
This part of her may last until the bell,
perhaps a year. A glance outside may tell.

Unbroken sunset across the silt plain
leans in the window, deriding all shapes,
knocking the shadows sideways once again.
Chalk dust solidifies two broken scapes
propped on the sill. Some day soon
that girl will find her shadow squat at noon.

And this one? She'll leave, now that she can,
to work for drinks, good lays and a night's rest.
And then she'll feel it in her bones how man
is easy straight up or flat out at best;
till at her gate one evening she will stand
watching his shadow deformed by ploughed land.

Single Ticket

The train rattles through the night.
That face opposite: more sallow now,
yet still that hair mists into light,
the skin more mobile on the brow.
A lapse of memory ... or time.
Gone that sidelong
glance her eyes had, green as lime.
Caught in scrutiny of a face,
they lowered like a dog's in disgrace.
Now tears rim those eyes once strong.

Time and again she glances my way.
Unsure, I wonder whether she tries
to place me or return the stray
stares I prolong to recognize
her features. I turn to the dusty pane,
and there's her face,
wrinkled and weeping in the driving rain.
Illness or years might make her look
like this. I nod back to my book,
returning through years to the old place.

A trick of memory, commonsense
insists. There's a ring on her hand.
Too much depends on coincidence
for one homecoming in years to land
me on this branch of the local line
in the same train
with her, however changed those fine
features, the laughter corded round
the lips.... I stare again as if bound
to catch some trait clinchingly plain.

That battered case offers no clue,
no name, no label. Travelling alone,
she troubles me like one I knew
by sight those years ago, the tone
of her voice unheard. I do not speak

23

and nor does she.
If once we'd broken week after week
of this we might have joined the train
together, and her eyes not show such pain.
I doubt it, though. She stares at me.

My stop. She gets out further down
the corridor and runs as once she ran,
when late, to catch her train to town –
or any woman runs to dodge a man
who eyes her too intently. I walk
the other way,
and two miles home, rehearsing talk
to come. Her heels tick into night.
– More faces to reshape at sight,
their recognitions to outstare next day.

Not Drinking Water

Home after years, tonight,
cleaning my teeth,
I taste the water of childhood,
still unfluorided,
tangless, not tepid, quite –
once an apple-slicing chill
by which all quenchings could be placed.

Suddenly minute fear,
not noticing the granary tower
by the old mill pond
that used to dominate the sky round here.
– Dwarfed
a little beyond
some concrete block for storing flour.

The water I've tasted:
shower, river, full of lime,
brine of the eyes,

sweat of her brow,
hard and soft and somewhere sour.
This taste I seem to forget.
I have been thirsty all my life.

Last Respects

I know these hands, their feel,
knew of the cuts beneath the scars
and wondered when the split nail would heal.

They used to lark
with birds of shadow on the wall
for children scared of the dark.

Fall now –
and all the birds are flown.

Hunched shadows black the wall.

Meditation Down the Wards

I look for some characteristic in each face
that marks them out for pain and sacrifice,
but they are all so different, some like myself,
so that I pass white-coated but unsafe.

Because there's so much agony to life
I would erect suffering into a belief,
make these men its martyrs and its saints,
and marvel at their useless innocence.

But just to state, though true, their pain is real
seems traitor, and to found on pain some rule
and order, callous. I'm a coward if I daren't
insist their pain's a pointless accident.

These faces do not change. They all are marked
by pictograms of grief, and they are mocked
by this pseudo-smile I try in fear and guilt,
to some response, though faked and difficult.

Passing the Gates

The fountain at the entrance in the square
with its thin dribble drizzling to the pool,
that I always hear when going anywhere,
today surprises me with silence, its drool
berged on the stone lit green by sun and slime.
Quiet recalls old Tom, the gateman, who'll
be thinking ice broke his thigh about this time.

Most doctors, picking up their mail, implied
he'd always need a stick. Yet summer came
and he was once more walking with his usual stride.
Fall came, and surgeons, checking all the same,
thought colostomy urgent. Trees gawked bare,
and somehow he was once more walking lame
when he returned to the fountain-drizzled square.

The impossible Pan, birdshot and tumbledown,
like an armless Deposition, drips once more
into my ears as I walk towards the town.
– Tap drips loudening to a roar
in restless sleep. I haven't visited
Old Tom. And now I stride on past the door
again, being afraid he might be dead.

Patient in a Ward

He holds his hand out like a sunflower drooping,
palm foremost on stalky wrist, the fingers
undone in dead petals hooking backward.

But this is no paper flower held waiting
in charity upon the street corners
to pass by with twopence or blank eyes lowered.

He is in pain. It is death thrusting
his hand out. – The desperation falters
seeing me reach for words of comfort.

The Visitors

They know no more than I would how to stand
with flowers, and, being men, sheepishly clutch
them, elbows stiffly bent,
as though a touch
of clothes or hand
would wither up the bloom and kill the scent.
They do not know the odd resilience of flowers.
They wait for wife's or child's visiting hours.

Shot on jets of green the tulips zoom
and weigh their stems across the corridors,
heavy and symmetric as eggs.
The visitors
need so much room
the trolleys brush the flowers or knock their legs.
They hinder the stretcher bearing one whose life
hangs in the balance. Someone else's wife.

Then for a nurse they thin to single file
and let her through to supper as though she rushed
to tend an injury.
Awkward and hushed,
they try a smile,
then shift and fidget, stood without dignity
at the beck and call of junior nurse or maid,
shielding their flowers, helpless, almost afraid.

Just Visiting

And you are one of these faces. At first
unseen, then recognized right down the ward.
A twitch of greeting since I couldn't wear
as far as that a smiling face, held fast.

You whine how much your cut hurts. You tell
me nurses forced you up to pack their wads
for sterilizing, made you decorate the ward's
long walls with flowers. And you quite ill.

I'm supposed to be horrified, to sympathize.
Yet nurses have to get the dressings done,
nightly have boys to lay and drinks to down,
like you, to make their leaving home worth this:

Sister's periods, the old and wrinkled faces
pursed on nerve-strings to the clenched lips,
hours of obedience enough to bring collapse
on hangover, and, then, cleaning up faeces.

And some of them have indolent golden hair.
Over there, a woman is dying, the line
of used laughter hung in bands on the lean
bones. And what you say I cannot hear.

I shudder. If your eyes started to glaze
I should listen now, although it could not lead
again to lively talk, drinks, light to slide
about your belly like brandy in a glass.

Such compassion couldn't save a grey hair,
not lift a hand. But you will live again,
and the living need a little love to go on.
You can speak now. I am here.

Obtainable from All Good Herbalists'

The eyes of your trinket laughter
are with me, they dance in the street,
like moon-skittering water;
I can hardly walk straight.

Oh what shall I do
with all these lights on route?
They will not distil a dew
to necklace your bright throat.

Hesitant, I halt
outside the herbalist's
for purslane and burdock held
to lengthen our lives and lusts.

Half-humorously I scan
the galleonate window bay:
julep, moly to gloss the skin.
Almost I enter and buy.

Yet if I bought a phial,
some glass-blower's masterpiece,
your health and joy to taste and feel,
that, after, as a vase would pass –

A careless wave of ease,
twin crescents of your laughter,
you'd flaunt before my face,
and then you'd drink plain water.

Sleek one, cultivate cats
with latex tongue and suede nose
for their flattering slinky coats.
Witch, you've taken my wits with your knees!

from THE MONTHS

Winter

All day I teach the children how thoughts are phrased.
I tell them there is beauty in our lives.

Across the playing fields the amber leaves
shine oldgold through the frost.

But, as the bus fills with their noise,
I gather my coat around me,
hoping none will call to me
and so transfer those looks that kill.

Snow and the leaves falling together.

The kids alight.
Then voices call attention
to a raincoat left behind.

I don't involve myself
to take and hand it back to her
next day at school.

(I shiver to recall some trip or other
I wept for something left behind as a child.)
A ten-year-old the weather hasn't chilled.
Snow and the leaves falling together.

And I relive the past weekend with her
sprawled like an old dress on the bed in tears.
And I with no tears to watch made for the stairs.

The draggled coat slumps here.

Thrush

Dawnlight hatches her cheeks with shadow lashes.
Thinking I'm still asleep
she draws my fist to feel how well
her flesh is hummocked with child.
I let her, playing fast asleep,
and don't unclench my hand.
She claws my fingers over her bared stomach.
They feel a bird,
as though caught in the hand,
tremble and flinch.

Gazing out of the window above my desk
I start
as something plummets from the eaves,
close to the glass in the dusk.
A tile, I think,
tensed for the thud as it dives.

But a thrush mounts up in flight,
beats down the garden,
banks to miss the trees, and greys
into night without trace.

Still tense for the thud,
I sit till quite late.

River-Garden

She sits drinking tea
in the river-garden,
a wing of hair
folded over her small ear.

Three packets of biscuits
she insisted on
tumbled like children's bricks
on the table here.

An eaveless tower of glass
rockets from shrubs behind her.
A pigeon comes to perch
upon her shoulder.

Across the table
a spring-heeled sparrow
bounces
in its search.

She breaks a biscuit
to draw them all around.
One of the bricks
already crumbles away.

She tries to aim the crumbs
at cheeky sparrows
but pigeons gather
and mill about the tray.

Another brick gone.
Now for the last.
– Ornithosis. Bird-shit.
Germ-ridden claws.

Useless to speak or say
she shouldn't feed them crumbs
because of swellings
they may cause.

Matchstick city clerks
stride to their trains
important
in their hurry home.

They glare in passing
at two provincials
who feed the daily pigeons
and block the thoroughfare.

Bats

Eight months gone,
               obsessed with birds,
at dusk she calls me to the window bay
to glimpse the fledglings trying out their wings
in grotesque flight
               in our room
reflected by the lamps.

               But they are bats.
Though, since her mind is turned to omens
and the old wives' tales she's heard,
I do not speak.
The cry of bats is tuned beyond our hearing
but a child's is not so hard.

from MORTAL FIRE

DEDICATION

to Pauline

*Your presence, love,
like the underlight
of trees within a wood,
that quiet pleasure
I could always predict,
often request.*

*But to tell you,
somehow share
this pleasure in writing,
always unbidden,
seldom predicted,
and solitary.*

*This you request of me
and I in return
promise to share
these ten years past,
yet find no words,
none like your presence.*

Walk from the House

I chanced to tread on a stag-beetle on the walk
from the house. It creaked like wickerwork.

But when you, father, fell and came to die
no detonation wrecked the streets that day.

A great matter went out of the universe
and nothing shook beneath its radiant force.

It should have knocked a world to stellar dust
but only a day or two my hands were dazed.

Yet now I watch my step in a distant town
as though a mine were buried at each turn.

Unaddressed Letter

I had no need to come to your funeral.
I heard the news only by telegraph.
The shock I felt was distant and unreal.
Nor was there with me one so aged with grief
to need an escort to the open grave.
A letter could have made my peace instead.
I had no need to come, yet there I stood.

Sheep on the hill like huge maggots. 'God shall wipe
away all tears from their eyes
and there shall be no more death to weep;
neither shall there be any pain or disease.'
– Something like that as mud sucked at my shoes.
I watched the watchers. But when ropes ran to inter
you there I saw a brown leaf give under a tear.

Now it is autumn and rain. Big drops you can trace.
I notice how one drop's enough to tear
an amber leaf out of the brittle trees.

I suppose much the same happened last year,
but it's now I notice, watching a caricature
of your face glooming over me as I stare
out of the window where the puddles stir.

The window reflects the galleon of fire still,
yards off in the dark, some useless knick-knack.
Rain drips regularly from the loose tile.
A wren ruffles the feathers round its neck,
sheltering in the gutter from the muffled knock
of continual rain.... Time to draw the blinds.
The galleon vanishes. A leaf zigzags as it lands.

The Fragments

My life must be Christ's broken bread,
My love his outpoured wine,
A cup o'erfilled, a table spread
Beneath his name and sign,
That other souls refreshed and fed
May share his life through mine.

Now they've returned by post the book of hymns
you gave me. It stands narrow among mine,
gold-backed and ribbed like bamboo-cane,
cleaner than the rest. You and your horn-rims
weren't given to read a line.
This music now and again
comes by me. Sometimes the words fill my head;
they speak with my desires but not your hope.
I try to change them for lines you haven't read.
With books you couldn't cope.

        'Grief fills the room up of my absent son ...'

They bring back evenings of study in my room.
Chords rolled from the organ keys you spanned,
the whole house empty. You couldn't read a bar,

only the tune and an octave's occasional boom.
Sometimes I couldn't stand
those wrong notes. They'd jar
your loneliness against me. I'd come downstairs
and make your supper and we would sit and eat
in silence separated by your stumbling airs,
and our eyes would not meet.

      'He talks to me who never had a son ...'

Erratic clack of typing rackets through
my room. Two-fingered my slow hands,
like feelered insects, pick at the crowded keys.
The duet, solos for two.
(A miner, trapped by land-
slide, tapping on his knees
to contact rescue.) But you're the buried one.
I know the ways between us, the walls and loosestrife;
letters unposted, journals in unison.
I'm the resurrection and the life.

      'He that would gain his life shall lose it ...'

– 'Being in the form of God, he thought
it not robbery to be equal with God
but made himself of no reputation and took
upon him the form of a servant and was brought
to the likeness of man ...' Your odd,
toby-jug figure shook:
' ... and fashioned as a man he humbled himself and became
obedient unto death, even the death
of the cross. Wherefore God hath given him a name ...'
And then you'd gasp for breath.

Strawlight stuffing poked from the bare light.
Crumpets of foam topped each icicled glass.
You entered the bar to sell your magazines
around the mellow; when they claimed their right
to hymns from bible class,
recalling childhood scenes,

I watched your hands fumble out some harmony.
You offered me your box. Coins would chink
in silence and you whisper: 'He that hath no money
come ye to the waters and drink ...'

6,000,000 Guinness drunk every day ...

And now I watch my hands fumble the keys
my type no better than your tunes – those short,
incurving little fingers, the family trait,
never to make the furthest stretch with ease.
How they skew and contort
to type at any rate.
Downstairs the strumming guts of guitars
and gramophones replace your wheezing tunes.
I watch acquaintances head for various bars.
The docile bus queue moons.

I watch them stand solemnly in that queue,
loaded with goods, without grimace or smile.
You'd handle them with tracts and pious books.
You'd always made out something you could do.
And now I watch them file
to see some film that looks
once more into the concentration camps.
This, how their victims queued, some accounts said.
Night falls. My face projects in the glow of lamps.
They move about my head.

6,000,000 ...

Radium Therapy

Deflated of flesh,
like axehafts,
the shinbones poke from rumpled bedding.

I hurry past
to avoid the radiation field.
The sweat and stench would make one retch.

But turn
to put the blankets straight.
And, leaning through the field,
I warm myself a little in my haste.

from HAVING NO ALTERNATIVE

'The sun shone, having no alternative, on the nothing new ...'
SAMUEL BECKETT: *Murphy*

Meeting

I would hardly have remembered your face
but then you used that strange word 'wayzgoose'
and it didn't seem out of place
in your Chinese-miniaturist choice of words.
Heard once it stayed in mind as your monogram,
recalled your Irish voice.

Then you left town
and I had this
as a memory of you,
this odd, misleading sound
for your medieval feasts of beer.

Returned unexpectedly after a year
you discovered someone relishing a word
you thought your own,
and in sheer delight now
you make him one to drink with here
but never bring to mind
how oddly this introduction was done....

Your dragonfly mind
hovered where seconds flower.

Courtesy Visit

In the small hours –
the din of voices in my ears –
you storm the stairs.

You reach my room for sanctuary
and drum upon the door,
then ram.

Almost in sleepwalk I open up.
You slump in,
weak, scarcely awake.

I turn the lock against them,
make Darjeeling,
black as you like it.

Cheeks veined with spider mauves,
your eyes blink slowly like fish mouths.
No muscle moves.

You've been on the drugs again.

The Terms

If I should suddenly hear that you were ill,
arrested or in need, I'd try to come
as soon as possible. And yet by rail
it still would take a day to reach your room.

If I should suddenly hear that you were ill
your letter would have taken a day to come.
You might be dead before I had the mail,
or die the day I travelled to your room.

And if I were unexpectedly taken ill,
I wouldn't write and trouble you to come
because I know you couldn't help, nor fail
to worry in your dark and curtained room.

This is our friendship. But still
you fled, maybe from this, and must have come
to fidget round some sleazy digs or jail
somewhere unknown ... or lie dead in your room.

You used to turn up suddenly with a will
in any old street. I miss the way you'd come,
that duffel winged out like a hawk, and hail
me through the traffic. Now streets are dumb.

Thinking of Writing a Letter

Now if I had your address what could I write?
I've seen the shots a cancer patient needs
towards the end. You drift incurably ill,
and your suffering must be worse, the drugs you take.

Suppose I said it's raining here tonight;
shared drinking yarns; sized up rival creeds;
let on I think of easy ways to kill
myself – but pills, not knives, the quarry lake.

They'd need courage. – Cold comfort that would make
in your despair. So I suppose I'd fill
some sheets with quotes, a rhyme, retort or slight
to draw you on to cap one of my leads.

And you would quote again that Yeats you take
to justify your ways beyond your skill.
Something like: 'Whatever flames upon the night
Man's own resinous heart has fed' it reads.

I see England mapped before me, dark and still,
and for a moment point after point of light
from every room you ever left succeeds
across it. The last melts out like a flake.

For twenty miles around there is no hill.
Time past for beacons that can reach your sight.
The silence of this water; jagged reeds;
lattice of light that lazy-tongs the lake.

Dear Murphy,

* * *

Separation

Because the night is cold
and I'm warm from your fire
I hurry down the road.

Yet, glancing back,
I see your shadow watching
at the upper curtains.

Before I wave
you turn into the darkened room.

Lullaby

Midges fizz in the dusk,
sky shows through a thin edge of moon,
a bit of honesty.

The night's a dark promise.
I can go no further with you now;
child, you must sleep.

Steps

I glance in at the open door
to see if my light disturbs you,
head and shoulders out of the covers,
abandoned, comfortable.

The sleeping beauty of children –
my mother's comment –
gushes over my childish head,
stalls my shadow on the floor.
I inch the door to.
Sudden dark might wake you.

Starting Your Travels

You try to outstare the journeying dark
but lights burst in heliographs that blind
your sleep-disfocused eyes:
a row of uprights falling to a car's
raking beams – like dominoes in file
or ranks in a crossfire.

The twin booms of light splinter like bars
of glass across your eyes. You look aside:
a horde of manoeuvring lights,
some market town in cover of the scarp.
That embrous mercury haze across the night
the way our route must lie.

Yet rest now, child. I see shapes in the stars.
And when you wake from dream in a few nights
for terror of the light
closing in round you from the black-moss dark
I shall know how to comfort you in time
and it shall comfort you in time.

Damages

Red admiral flickering by the cherry tree.
I saw those markings last when still a boy,
and shout, too sharply perhaps, for you to see –
afraid insecticides may soon destroy
the last before you see your first one drift
among the phlox and sideslip, dither, lift.

And, dropping toys, you hurry to my room
fearfully fast and stand almost in tears.
(It's darning up the garden, bloom to bloom.)
I point and out you dart. It nears, then veers,
now poises like a gnomon. Caught in the end.
You bring it me dead; its wings I cannot mend.

Thwarted, I try to explain calmly, brush
the vivid dust from your hands. Still you insist
it fly again, persist, and will not hush
until my angry tone conveys the gist
of death. Silenced, you give me the crumpled wings;
I shelve them with your heap of broken things.

But not till bedtime dare you bring the car,
Buick Riviera with plastic conduction lights,
dropped, when I'd called you, on its towing bar.
You have the pieces. I say I'll put it right.
The tears delayed this morning drop as I take
the glowing plastic glue will turn opaque.

Sleep well.
           Your toys, my books cobble the floor.
There's that Lagonda I bought myself as a boy.
Toys to repair clutter my desk and drawers.
Irreparably damaged some you most enjoy.
Here since you insist on repairs. Instead,
my words and promises litter your head.

Your strength beyond your skills, so fast you grow;
I cannot clear the backlog of things you break.
More complex now your gifts; already, though,
technology in your toys outstrips me. I make
this pile, your broken marvels, forgotten, outgrown.
My words and ways you may not so simply disown.

Full Circle

Same book. Last year the reader's throat grew dry,
the meaning garbled till the mood was lost
on all the rest in boredom. This time I'll read
the ending out: their prison-ship is tossed
against the rocks of home; one friend must die
saving the younger just as both are freed
from chains by storm to grasp the chain of hands
that friends reach out across the years and sands.

'Greater love ...' Yes. Even that quote.
That faithful girl has kept a light lit there
for seamen in such straits! Now home, the dead
hero is laid out on the table where
he once had laid his son in death. And note:
the son adopted mourns the father dead –
a careful symmetry. And one attends
them, grey-haired now, not knowing his old friends.

– I ham it up. The seniors I overlook
glance up from private study, grin: the course
they did two years ago. They catch my eye
but other eyes are reddened by the force
of words, and blinkered by their tears to the book,
for hero's death when nearly home and dry;
for one, after long exile returned. Neat,
unlikely, a vicious circle so complete.

Lump in the throat. Yet not for hero friends,
still less for home that circles round once more,
nor for the woman who could wait so long
for love; but for impossibilities of this order,
coincidences needed to shape these ends –
seniors listening now; for kids so strongly
moved by the frame of life prefigured there.
– The seniors already know it will not wear.

'Finis.' And silence. I must break this spell.
Seniors laugh off the mood remembered, lame
laughter the kids can hardly understand.
Try questions. No one answers. Pick a name.
A laugher or a quiet one?... The bell.
And out they file too quietly. A handful
of seniors asks how many times the book
comes round. Half-smiling, I answer with a look.

Thirty Summers

Clouds shift; the shadows fall.
Stallion-gloss of sunlight
on a bough-back.

Clouds shift; the leaves rustle.
I wait for that sunshaft
to light there again.

Terrace

A terrace of tulips
colourful as a crowd.
What they need
is a match to watch.

Will this old tabby do,
sleeping in the sun?

Crowd

Come away from crowds,
you fool;
why do you hang about?
If she should turn up now
she would be old.

That one is like her, dark,
long hair,
strong stride, unshaken calf ...
Unfaithful eye,
recharge the memory.

Old Poet on a Rainy Day

FOR DAVID JONES

My old acquaintances and peers
once allied in the lonely art
and rivals in our riper years
gather together now on shelves
after so sure a life apart
and peace becomes their books, themselves.

THE GOING

Wait and See

This is the bar you said where we could meet.
I take the corner opposite the door,
prepared to wait
and half-resigned to sit
with one glass for an hour.

Each time a figure darkens the window
I watch the door. And for a moment
a head takes on that bob of yours,
a leg your casual lope,
and I am drawn by you
to several other women.

Tangibles

It was one of those autumn days,
you said,
as if they were consecutive,
distinct yet somehow comparable
as the misty shimmer in each pearl
around your throat.
And so I remember it was –
the crack of apple,
the tang of juice in the teeth
and your hands
always cold to first touch.

Country Walk

I've wound it many times
around my fingers,
that scroll of your hair
fumbled over by the breeze.
It will carry these buttercups
and more.

Masses of buttercups
blacken the grass
until we walk unsteadily
a sky of shaking stars.

Down to earth
in our old spinney,
the sun a hole charred in the boughs,
you reach across me
seeking a leaf of every green
till I catch
in the tips of your hair
a spectrum of stars.

The Swifts

The swifts are back,
their flight on a knife-edge.
In the dusk we watch them
and feel at peace.
Their grace we take
for confirmation.

Our swifts are back,
we say, and touch now.
But their grace survives them,
whichever were ours.
And it hurts to touch you,
that wing of hair.

Whose love, my love,
in my hands tonight?
Whose spring again
in the bounce of your hair?
Our love is ghosted;
our swifts return.

Silver Birch

A delicacy of white feathers
that can cut the hand
rising out of the mist.
One bough the leading edge
of a swan's wing raised for flight.

My hands could span the trunk
arched into darkness
like your throat
thrown back in love.

One dusk when mist returns,
walk along this way, love,
gather an inkling,
my angle of you,
your head thrown back.

Presence

Shadow of a bird in flight
across my window
jogs my room like a blink.

A whole train of thought gone
as though you with your quiet
had come in and sat down.

Returns

A few silver birches among dark pines
like frozen lightnings. They take us back.

You tried to match your steps to my prints
in the soft earth here, such strides.
You pranced in those days. But look,
I cannot tread again in my last print.
A minute edge crumbles like those cliffs
at Cromer where we walked ten years ago.

The going loosens. I take your wrist once more.
White pressure of my grip expands
more or less the same as when you first
stumbled on these tracks
although I cannot touch you quite again
where once I held you fast.

We cover the same ground.
Your life fits into mine.

Dusk

Moon a sliver of apple
blue on a knife-blade.

Light enough for a known face.
I touch shadow round your eyes.

Gift of Words

That patience of yours,
standing half the morning
to watch a rose you planted bloom.

So long like that, years,
you've waited for me.
I have to watch you always.

Crescent of melon, your bare back
where blouse and jeans have come apart.
The windows between us.

Too impatient to watch your roses,
I want my hands to feel
the equipoise of your hips.

You turn with a spray of roses,
a focus for my room,
fragrant cloud, I think you call them.

The petals will drop silently for days,
scented on these files and folders.
Sometimes I've heard them land.

Crocus

Our old gnarled path.
We're late again this year,
the still flame in our clump
of crocus past its best,
but one, sculptured, fragile,
half an eggshell.

Your head to one side,
your hair heavy and slow,
my plumb-line,
sways to the vertical
as you kneel and try
to purse it up to flame again.

Sleep

As soon as your sleep is sound
I slip my arm from around you.
You can't tell
though you'll dream something up
to explain your loss of warmth.

In the still hours
your cold hands reach for me.
Their gentle pressure
hardly disturbs my sleep.
Unstirring, they become my warmth.

Lullaby

Sleep, love, go to sleep
and I'll watch over you
as I have done these years,
these shadows of curtain haze,
and breathe into your hair
the things we do not say.

You murmur as if you hear
some saying of the day,
and nuzzle the pillow down,
but, tracing an edge of light
along your shoulder line,
my hands touch on your dream.

Hold

That perfect apse,
your fingers with their curvature.
They hold a stillness
I can't touch.

Tentative,
your hands sense out
for things as if air
lay denser round them.

Mine
that undo things for you
would leave their mark.
Love,
it's not much
but it's something
we hold together.

Lost and Found

The warmth of her, unbreathable
as she presses over me
hopelessly scanning the shelves
the only way she knows.

(She asked the time on Westminster Bridge.)
She turns the plants to the sun
and she is looking for a map of the district.
I round on her – like a moth.

Old Haunt

Scotch fir, the trunk
staked in the still pools of its boughs
on the old hill.

The needles kill the grass
where we left our shapes
so long ago.

Its criss-crossings
crazed your bare legs.
You tried for a fern pattern.

This stillness was there then;
boughs like green snow overhanging;
and the peace was no trouble to us.

Two Sparrows

They take off squabbling
and loop each other
like a flying bolas –
and their shadows.

Time to see it happen:
our hands like that now
when they skirmish to manoeuvre
in open tenderness.

Gifts

More books,
that dress I thought was you,
worn once,
another pen to try my hand.

We're down to gifts now,
mine against yours,
and each more costly than the last.

They hang fire about us everywhere.

Meander

Dark meander of hair
a river between banks of snow
and my touch lasting
like a snowflake in its course.

Keeper

Something about you that might break,
a hand's turn,
delicate as a figurine,
caught and held me.

Something small and terrified
sheltered in the verve of your eyes
like a silver fox,
nocturnal, svelte.

A lull in the talk,
the dark suddenly noticeable
and the odd glance
of something too timid to tame.

The sight grows rarer, love.
It keeps more and more from me.
My old nightfarer,
let it still live.

Retrospect

Wanting some yourself
you offer me cherries.
Girlish again
you hang a pair over your ear
pale where they touched
as your breasts were.

Wanting memories
you hold out a wishbone stalk
to split between us.

But I want my time back.
Give me back
the pressure of my hands.

Tie

A marbling of fine veins
across your right temple,
the skin opalescent.
Blood too near the surface.

Truce

In your play which was no play
the knife glanced my arm,
a red mouth opened mute.
A fortnight's casual conversation
out of that
now healed to a scar.

Twilight

Dusk
lit by a bowl of roses
and your hand white, so white
against the oak table,
poses a peace I know only by sight.

Dark to you always
my hands seemed closer once

than nocturnes in black and white
those nights your shoulders gleamed,
that mane of shadow down your back.

Deadlock

Nothing more irritating
when the hands are engaged
than a trickle of liquid
like an insect running down the face,
rain or sweat or even blood.

You want me to take your hand in mine
and will not want to dry your eyes
until I do,
though I will wait
until you fall asleep.

Impasse

Your eyes closed on me.
Your drift always against my drive.
I draw your scalp back by the hair
to lift the lids.

And by the time they do
I shall have gritted my teeth
into a smile for you.

Retraction

Your overnight bag gone;
so much left behind:
you tried to keep everything.

I go over again in black
the words I wrote to you
or underscored in red.

The flourishes defeat me,
the dab hand
has lost its cunning.

The red shows through.
I'll send them on.
Retraction enough.

Insight

For sight like an ophthalmoscope,
once it was a wish,
now what a hope,
to penetrate the leaf-light
of your green iris
to the shadow-play beyond.

The dark can take you now
for all a shaft could show:
a room of gipsy flowers
and potted plants,
the ten-mirror echo
of your defensive laugh.

Keepsake

You call me to you
kneeling over a single crocus
under the oak.

Your scroll of hair
now screening the steady flame,
some secret you'd have unique:

These three impressures
inset within the petal,
fluted, concave, minute.

How long we'd keep this insight in season,
you said,
as ours, strong as a vow.

But I have held that moment:
you leaning,
your hair scrolled around your shoulders.

And now this clump of crocus
hidden a moment in time,
its saffron blinding.

The Mind's Eye

Curls that should jingle with your slightest move –
I might have known you'd soon be back,
your next shift
to trouble the mind's eye.

Naked, or dressed to kill.
But clothed – that's new.
I watch the passes that you make,
your hands slow-motioning to save a glass.

Your skirt deflating like a parachute,
you kneel and tilt your head
to catch the glint of fragments littering the floor.

That skirt's a laugh,
and just to pique you more
I'm going to make you last like that
and unaware before me on your knees.

Those curls will jingle at your slightest move –
After-image, my after-love, look up.
You're still my only source of feeling.

Eidetic Image

Memory of a girl laughing,
your hair a fall of flame,
gold burning down
and shadow flickering up,
head to one side
like a bird listening.

Pose of an advert now –
mirror enough for you at last –
you get at me from all angles.

I don't know how widespread you are
but I expect you everywhere.
And at this distance alone reflect –
nostalgia if you like –
that maybe you never posed this one before,
a girl laughing in her glass
without your famous poise,
the shadow flickering up,
the gold burning down.

Obsession

I bear you in mind always – white
as balsa wood your body was.
You were all women once to me.

The blade of shadow down your thigh,
it's pretty common; some of your ways
I love in every woman I meet.

I've assembled them all tonight,
all dressed to kill and all to watch
your private strip; it's your big scene.

I bare you in the mind's eye
so make it hot and strong for once;
they'll take your fine points off, my sweet.

Vigil

Now you are gone
your small perfections inveigle me:
curve of your eyelid closed in sleep
widens to my horizon.

Sleepless
I used to watch those pupils move,
shifting deltas of blue veins,
blindly scanning my face.

Some nights I came near,
my lips in touch
with your pulsing lids
to catch the drift of your dream.

Wild Flower

Crushed fragrance
and a few flower heads
bend to the light
out of my footprints –
purple florets,
established, wild,
encroaching underfoot.

How long ago it must have been
you told me the local name
for something much like this,
if I remember it,
in those days
when what your hands touched
was my life.

from **CROSS CHANNEL**

Recognition

Face once loved,
so constant in the mind,
I could have passed you anywhere
not knowing who you were.

Rain

All morning long now, missing you,
I sit and watch the summer rain
falling, ticking through the shrubs
against the window – white blooms.
You would know their country names,
these flowers you would never cut.

And there beneath the leaves that give
some delicate filigree of grass,
blunt pencil's double line its stem.
One drop would break it down if hit.
But minutes of this time have passed
and not a drop has nicked it yet.

The tip-down of a neighbouring leaf
gives it a momentary, brushing shock –
one bulging drop about to fall
left globed upon its filigree.
The leaf recoils, smashes the drop.
The rain pours. I watch that stalk.

You would know its country name.
You always knew what to call
those unseasonable costly sprays
I brought to make your tears my fault.

Unspoken

This ache always to bring you
a gift to last some time
and yet I know
how this would go beyond the drift
of our arrangement:
flowers or food,
wine to persuade a share of mood.
That's how we've got it made.

And anything much beyond these
would be in time the gift for loneliness
and let you press the same on me,
some token lasting thing
until all we have now,
these late daffodils,
would somehow be over.

ONE ANOTHER

A Sonnet Sequence

FOREWORD

This sequence of sonnets springs from an obsession with the solipsism of experience. Friends have implied that there is too much of this in the poems and that a few remarks to clarify the narrative would hardly come amiss. The story, simple, if not tenuous, is of a couple in love over a period of years. Their relationship is seen intermittently from either point of view; the octave-sestet division is sometimes used to mark the change. From the first sonnets where the man revisits his old village, through the obsessive and possessive emotions of love, the time passes into mature experience, reflection and death. The motive power of several sonnets is provided by the man's assumption that he will die first, whereas the woman does. She is driven by a search for the unique whereas the man is obsessed by the cyclical nature of most experience.

I cannot say more; the sequence is the morphology of an emotion – always more varied than language would have us believe – and it must change for the reader also as he or she becomes aware of the echoes and interrelations between lines and poems.

I should not like to end this note without recording my gratitude and thanks to Kenneth Crowhurst and Humphrey Clucas who read the manuscript and offered valuable advice and reactions.

P. D.

The Lane

The willows hang their yellow swarms across
the turning by the humpback bridge – that lane.
I still can make the river wash and swirl,
sucking the stonework underneath, and feel
pocking the wall-top the green grit of moss.
Like scratches down old movies, a thin rain.
No one turned there, not even boy and girl
in all the years I passed. It's almost real.

I shan't walk now along that nameless lane.
(Only the memory pays for local maps.)
No face or place in the village to take me back.
Posit: the first aerial, then the stack,
a few houses expecting no one perhaps,
a child wondering away, nose to the pane.

Landscape

Me peeling away at a loose end of bark,
the silver birches; there, the stunted one,
a run of silver paint on rough grained wood,
and underfoot the usual dumping ground.
That childish hope when this was more a park
to peel some silver off and catch the sun
or make a mirror. Never any good.
But here's a trunk my hands can still surround.

Me peeling away at a loose end still,
watching the darkness grow beneath my hand,
scorched earth, scorched earth, and, staring in my face,
the old landscape I thought I left at will.
– Eyes, eyes that bear in mind this meagre land,
look back; hold me stronger than the place.

Dissolve

Face of a Greek tyro, and the neat hair
a cap of sparrows' wings, the lean thigh
in motion scooped and fluted, midriff bare –
I look for what it is that takes my eye,
and wish you deftest screw and steady aim
for no good reason but the longbow curve
your leg has, tensed; supply you with a name,
moth to a flame, that dark central reserve.
A sleepless night I had of it, your taut
body still poised to cue, your face, that face
pursuing, not pursued, in every thought.
And then a name clicked back into its place.
      Hard, to recall how long ago things last,
      my love, old love, my stand-in for the past.

Response

Dear, I should like you once in your life to be moved
by a printed phrase, not for the writer's sake,
still less for mine, but so that you could say
for once how odd it feels to learn your mood,
your feelings nursed along so nice and lush,
are nothing private to speak of, nor quite fresh,
my love, my dearest love. Though do not fret
yourself; there's something here to like or lump:

The dead tabby's paw clatter on the glass
when rain or shadow trick the eye, odd times,
can shake me more than what the mind replays
of one with her Shetland-pony fringe and glance,
or, worse, the moccasin-slouch, palm-forward style,
of that one from my student days, the plague.

Cone

Not dearest, but the nearest I have come
to love, such as it is, I'll watch you read,
your urchin hair within the lamp light's cone,
the spray arrested on those curls that screen
your face. I always fell for that, but more
a street light's cone, I don't know why, in rain,
an auburn head, the storm's panicky morse,
the lamp light and a moment's ambered grace.

No, don't look up, my love, nor ask with eyes
what if we had our time again. Read on,
calves under thighs, your knees like new loaves,
and let me see you read my thoughts tonight:
the busby neatness of that auburn gone,
our destination dark and undisclosed.

Dialogue and Soliloquy

'Let's talk about the roses. They don't hurt,
do they? Red, spiky – red or maroon?
Soft, aren't they soft? And quite inert.
And look, there, look: the silly old moon
gormlessly dithering like a kid's balloon
left on a pond. That cloud making it spurt.
The darkness comes. Let's talk about it soon.
A snug fit, a shade closer than your skirt.'

– I am the apple of his inner eye.
He wants to core me and he bores me, bores.
Once in a blue moon I'm two in his sky.
Cowish, I jump them for him on all fours.
I'm strip lighting and he wants it stark:
'Nearest, you come no closer than the dark.'

A Little Light

Once it was a touch and then a tone of voice
and always promise of a turn of mind.
I could have touched your lashes any time
and you not bat an eyelid nor recoil.
Such calm. Your trust was always hard to take.
We've colonized a space now, an arm's reach,
filled with the things we touch on, books I need,
the plants you tend, green-fingered, self-contained.

Pressure, a touch, it never took much to work;
gentleness, warmth, the shadow mask on eyes
that give back nothing but a little light.
You turn from me, you grope for timeless words
and my dumb hands go out to you in time
to hold, like a flower's scent, your mind in mine.

The Rose

Such concentration on a single rose,
you look as though you watch it breathe the scent
till I am watching you and held intent,
your breath so hushed it hardly comes or goes.
What does it say to hold you in that pose,
that my lips cannot move, my hands invent?
Your words, they never tell me what is meant;
my hands can't touch the peace your body knows.

Pale bloom that gathers light from dusk, your hand
as white as whittled hazel without shine,
the sill and window where you hold quite still.
A word could break the spell.... I ache to stand
in for your eyes and grasp this rose in mine
as closely as your hand along the sill.

Insights

When shall we ever know each other more
than you this rose or me this quietude
of yours that breathes a presence through the room,
your slightest movement making stillness clear
as flickers of the firelight do. You pore
over the vase. You wouldn't know my mood,
nor I your insight to a rose's bloom;
your rose a focus, mine a misting sphere.

Move, love; finger the petal fallen there.
(Your palate's curvature, its touch to me.)
Now feel the micro-hesitance and know
the sense my hands have of your skin – your hair,
more like, that rounds their roughness in its flow.
So touch the rose, and in my hands you'll be.

Record

It is her microphone. She speaks with powers
I do not hear, no movement on her lips.
Dumb rose, record her thoughts, her fingertips
for after-comers. Make her the language of flowers.
– No, no, she listens. Others murmur here.
This is the poise that I have never caught.
To let go of a rose as of a thought,
the bloom untremored as her hand lifts clear.

Are roses still becalmed where Helen is?
The trees drop shadows; light ripples the leaves.
That time, held frame, of shadeless memories;
the light like glass. Oh, love, you turn again.
If only we let go as your hand reprieves
a rose, unmarked, and the daylight could be plain.

Talisman

Bell-flowers, seldom seen now, stellar, trim,
on porcelain where the day is warm and clear
as flame within a candle's melting rim;
that squirl so delicately fellowed here.
– The trinket-well I gave you long ago
to cast a wistful spell that was your own.
And it became you, love. But now it's broken,
my clumsy hands: the light flawed with a mote.

It hurts, as if a talisman, now drained,
withdrew its gentle aura from you, though
you're just the same and do not seem aware.
But here's the perfect match at last obtained.
Throw out the first and who would ever know?
Yet no two days of summer make a pair.

Match

Someone who loved the clay and loved the flowers
made this and caught the look of day in it.
Not one who tried to see how exquisite
it was in loving me and my sad hours.
The broken one I'll save as rightly ours
and you will sometimes see me watch that split
and blur it out with wondering how we knit
our days together with such clumsy powers.

Someone who loved me gave this broken thing
and I will match it with the perfect one.
These two shall be for us a perfect match:
one past and one to come, as time may bring.
And since we don't know which of them is done
we may move gently and perfection snatch.

Silence

Cloud stilted along on two great spokes of light.
And then to enter the room, its shadow cool.
A bowl of roses, the oak table, white blooms
like slow swans reflected in its pool, plumes
brushed by a moment's breeze. A dusty gold
fizzing a shaft of sun, the mullion's shade
leading across the carpet – shoulders bare,
shadowed by a great silence of cascading hair,

the woman sitting, focused within her mind,
(myself unseen) hands folded in her lap
cupping the darkness loosely like a bird,
book on the floor accordioned.
                                To find you there,
presence to presence. Cloud happens to change
the light. You turn as though you heard it move.

Declination

That momentary declination of your head,
the water-chevron hairs along your nape,
revive an old attraction. I slowly drape
your shoulders, hold you there. You turn instead
your baffled squirrel look – and nothing said,
all lost. My love, some day I'll buy a cape
and every time your hair's in its great shape
I'll help you on with it to bow that head.

What binds us, dearest, is this touching grace.
It's like a cat's or in a squirrel's leap.
Or else, for me, the glossing of a beech.
But you know the dodge, the time and place.
I have to eavesdrop on your style of sleep –
your eyelids close and you are out of reach.

Aubade

Our hands have had their say time and again:
your quiet touch, the cat in the dog's shade,
a sneaking stroke of love in the shopping parade,
some grasp of shared experience in pain.

Dark in my long watch of your summer sleep,
I wonder what my hands would have to say
the day you die. And all the words that weigh
into the head make my flesh and blood creep

to you to wrest you closer from the night.
– Sleep on, my love, sleep in your cool bed.
May these cold hands never enter your head.
And in the morning may the breaking light
suffuse your lids with rose before you wake.
The first shadow on you my touch will make.

Shadow

Shadow of a leaf on a butterfly's wing,
solid as a beetle's wing-case, fine veneer.
I wait to hear it click down like a spring

the instant that the tortoise-shell flits clear.
I'm learning to be patient, love. You freeze.
My hold is less than light on you, that sheer

absorption, as you tense for flight or breeze.
Glacially, you edge forward now. I know
enough of you to see you mean to ease

your shadow over the wing and hold it so.
That daft stray lock of yours will almost reach.
You cannot make it stay. It's touch and go.

The shadow leaf snaps down in me like a screech.
I catch you off balance and without speech.

View

So much, so much ... I only have to reach
my hand to you, my fingers swaying the fine
hair of your nape as the breeze that field of wheat.
You hardly notice, though there comes to mind
a gentle lulling. And this pressure to hold
your mind to instances of mine – it seems
almost enough. These hands can trail a shoal
of lights along your hair and you will sleep.

And I would hold the gift of sleep for you.
– No other gift so good, unless some tact
were in my hands to press on you the mood
of this great purple thunder-bank, flint-knapped
along the brink with light, or to attune
my sense of music to your stone-calm hands.

Music

Full of mortal longing the cor anglais yearns.
I thought of Chatterton, the marvellous boy,
at least that painting in the Tate, the light
there, or that *April Love*, the rich mauves,
the light there much the same, as she half turns
and looks inward. Her song would surely cloy.

> An English wood and autumn burning late,
> the boat-knock branches as the light breeze moves,
> those kipper-coloured leaves and, feather-frail,
> one poplar. The pile of this moss so smooth,
> so cool to stroke. A squirrel, brown, ears frayed,
> quizzical; sun enough to make him muse.

His reaper sang contralto in this cadence.
Will no one tells me what she hears, my music?

Her Concentration on a Nutshell

They used to make us cockleshells for the bath.
You open them so gently, knife down the seam.
Uncrinkle the kernel, though. What worlds of earth
would round out from the walnut; not the same,
oh, not the same as ours! Another scale.
The mind it is, inside the head. (He'd like
to crack my codes, edge deep into the skull.)
I part the hemispheres with a nuclear click.

Colour of blanched almond, these firm thighs,
and curved the same where they surface in the bath.
This English pallor, smooth and hazed. – All space
is curved and he has reached his bound in these.
He wants me all and he can have them both.
Come, tan of walnut juice, you add some spice!

Pressed

These flowers are a gentleness in my grasp.
My hands harbour the haft-hold too long,
their lightest drift to you a weathered rasp.
These slight flowers give as the wind grows strong.

This wide reach of evening, all that surf
of cloud-rack, the thunder-bank's great rift,
the rayless sun no more than a clean pine kerf.
Flowers and hand one shadow on the drift.

See, we could press them there against your skin
and mine, mementos of our day – though much
the better in a book. Words always win.
We'd have to stay like this all night in touch.

– Love, in your most private grief, my hands
have never touched you without desire to have.

Sunset and Storm

Cool grass-blades creep up and over my hand.
The old blaze of sunset deepens the thunder-bank
on green-tops wet with light, liftless, tranquil.
All's said and done, my love. You understand,
the years I have assumed, this peace before storm.
(Eye blinked by the wingless flight-phase of a bird.)
This wait that never varies for leaves stirred
by the first gust, the first rain, chill, enormous.

Too long I've let these things speak for me.
I can survive only as long as your mind.
Hold instances of mine. This bracelet of bone
that splays your hand in the drenched grass. You're free.
Go in. Wash off the mud. But leave behind
the link of skin that binds you in your own.

Deed of Gift

It's not enough. Not personal enough.
Landlubbers all have fallen for this time.
Something that pulls the mind up sharp like a lime,
I need, none of this sentimental stuff.

I'll give you a pendant watch. It's not much
but wear it always under your blouse to tell
a moment you can only show yourself.
It will take your breath away, cold to the touch.

I'll clip the catch for you. Nod down your neck,
hold still. But my hands, love are cold, so cold.
There now. Your pulse is beating the time told.
I promise you'll only hear the odd second

like a skipped beat: my hands chill on your nape
and your thin skin cringing up like crape.

Shades

My hand's reach larger than life upon the blind,
the light so limited that the dark leaks in.
You shudder at the shape in mind, you say;
a branch wuthered against the window, bare,
hag-black to stifle you – until my hand,
soft as a shadow, brushes away your cry.
Dark promises, my love, lie candid there.
I've just the ghost of a touch to sidle down
your spine. Once a shadow, always a ghost.
Remember among windswept oaks or cloistral beech
these hands. They'll haunt your body mostly there.
How they'll remember at arm's reach you comb
      and slowly comb your hair until it gleams
      satisfactorily with my sweat. Sweet dreams.

Moon

These hands are so old. I don't know what to think.
They hold their own when I have lost my grip.
They know of ways around that you let slip.
You tremor like water just above the brink.

I watch your face for thoughts, for mood – your face
wizened a moment by movements soft as time.
Look, love, I'll gather what your features mime.
Your eyes reflect a light I cannot place.

Now you are young again. In the low light
your skin-tone has the mother-of-pearl that blurs
the rimless moon in mist. That's the rare sight
you always bring to mind now, though you smile:
and what if that means frost and heavy furs?
You'd lie there still, my love, in all your style.

Frost

White crystals clear, lean over, melt away
as breath peels back along the frosted fence.
Moss-feints return. The wonder is all day
whether the grain, the green, will be as dense
when dusk returns, or white again with frost,
clinging like iron filings, to the wood.
Again he breathes his warmth, all focus lost,
until the knot nets outwards as it should.

– So much you bring back as you bend, your hair
brushing the frost, and breathe to melt the white
upon a spider's web, taking good care
to break no thread. More frost, my love, tonight.

Like kids, my lips will melt a frost tonight,
a frost and frost of light along your lids.

Hand and Head

I sweat it out, your perfume in the heat;
the closest we have come, and dear enough
without this hankering for the deeper stuff.

And yet to know you like an open book,
my lost language never glossed completely.
You turn over again to a clean sheet.

Just once, perhaps, to read of my approach
under the cover of your sharpest lookout
calmly anticipated nook by nook.

In these arms also your need of surprise,
a stroke of genius rather than encroachment,
the craft say, of this fronded silver brooch.

– 'King Alfred ordered me made.' – How neat it lies,
a starry blur above foreshortened thighs.

The Shadow

She promised all. You gave me what you had:
your stillness centripetal to a room,
your gawky poise coaxing a rose to bloom,
barefoot, your heel-down, ballerina pad.

And yet you can't compete within her shadow.
In dreams, in anger, she surfaces, assuming
a sleeking otter-back of naked grooming
under the nylon, its flowing off so gradual.

Breast turning a propeller of light, she straddles
her stole, manoeuvring for the slowest zoom-in.
– That once you stalked off in the pine-dark gloom
and she turned up in only your old plaid.

Bare, with your heel-down, ballerina pad,
your bird-launching laugh, how she skedaddled!

A Long Shot

Mad hikes over bracken, nettlebeds, wildflowers
to find a place no foot had trodden first.
I swore I'd remember every single hitch
but in the end you were too many for me.
You always were impossible. A place all ours,
there must be one, you say.
      A struck tree,
the boggiest corner, midges at their worst,
its riven trunk straddled across the ditch.

Just as it fell, you say, the storm last night.
You have to walk on it in your high heels.
Your flared skirt of blinding saffron peals
this way and that, my silent bell. One stone,
then you strap-hang on a willow, a real sight.
Hold it.
   And here you stand on tips of bone.

The Thunder Stone

Ten years and no memories to call our own,
you say, eyes scavenging across the field,
raking the skyline for something it might yield.
(Basket creak of leaves by the dry-stone.)
Let's find a gap that no one else has known
and get an angle frost or wind revealed,
then with a seeded handful of earth concealed,
or cones – my sparrows drying off, windblown.

– No, here's a chalky flint I split on flint;
our landscape on its surface and, inside,
these mirror-image, thunder-purpled skies.
All glint, and water will restore the glint.
They'll never fade to blue. This one we'll hide,
the other take – a match that never lies.

Storm

Your fear of lightning, my need of the storm.
The great pylons a pale shadow of the cloud
bouldered above us and your slight figure cowed.
Sky cracks like ice and the rain slow and warm.
Your hand in mine. I cannot hold your fear
and you can't draw the need from me, your head
so close I muffle up your other ear.
The two of us, you say, the two of us dead.

The power to drive a city in that flash,
all spent to burn a vacuum in the sky.
I watch it branch and you tense for the crash.
Big drops darken and connect across your dress.
Love, where we hold close we are bone-dry;
you cling, and what comes through is powerless.

Walk

I know, I know. It is only a dream,
but there are dogleg rivers I cannot cross
and paths in company I walk alone:
a certain tilt of willow, a touch of moss.
Yet still there come these moments when you seem
some distance with me in the placeless zone –
unless I catch sight of the knurled bough
angling the path I cannot quite say how.

Though, love, you must have paths and paths to walk.
How you might need my hand to bring you through.
(That flint split to a sky of thunder grey.)
And you might reach for me as now you do
and say: 'That's betony, that broken stalk,
and that chink-chink's a thrush. They fix the day.'

Bird's Eye

We take an hour off in the watery sun.
Bird's eye, you suddenly exclaim: minute,
a tiny pansy-type of a bleak blue.
I actually like the thing, the way it shuns
the eye, less brash than pansies.
                              Not the name,
you say, my mother called it that. You find
the name. It must be in the books.
                                    I'll try,
love, though we know it's just to pass the day.

I'll find its name, and it will be the name
of that nothing we did to say we lived.
But bird's eye, let the children say
until, when grown, they find its grassy dip
and wonder over what its true name is.
– Birsy, love, the flower I cannot change.

Memento

A leaf. He's given me an autumn leaf,
faded, but never to perish with the fall.
The marvels of technology! Every least
serration, every vein and slightest fault
precisely sealed in burnished copper foil,
and yet so light. He'd even make a style
of dead leaves. I'll wear it over the void
of my breast. There, leaf to the closest eye.

Funny this catch.... And there's a pinpoint leak
the foil has left. The air will seep inside.
Brave new technique, and he has not the skill
this time to mend it. Slowly, slowly, leaf,
you'll sidle out on me, his secret sign,
built-in obsolescence of life under a skin.

One Another

I am that silent pool. I mirror, opaque.
I float the water lilies, candescent flame,
and I reflect the imperturbable swan.
No cloud-race scuffs my surface; that stake
lays claim to my depths, leaving no wake.
Minnows dart bright silence, the perch aim.
Stones make rings around me and are gone.
I still the rain's trickle. I become a lake.

Her body flows from me in the night.
Like evening mist on a river, she comprehends
the darkness. As blossoms in the mist, the white
to white, my touch floats down to her and ends
somewhere unseen, drifting with the stream.
The fearful silence where dark waters gleam.

Dream

Your presence like a drug that does no harm
cannot enclose me from the trackless night.
Let me sleep now ... and your pervasive calm.
– Awareness hurtling down a rail of light,
it plummets headlong in the roaring ditch
where bones, a mildew green, clutch out their roots,
and blood seeps from a wound this stolid pitch
of ants that waver to yowls of distant brutes.

Let us rest now, love. The terror will keep.
Only in nightmare is it safe to scream.
All quietudes I have you manage to find;
I will not promise you my share of sleep.
Still waters widen the quiet in your dream.
Let us sleep now; the dark is to my mind.

Compact

For term of life you are determined mine.
Some tree is bound to shadow forth my reach:
no man whose hand has not the same design;
a touch or two of mine you'll have to teach.

And when you seek the years in the window pane,
a dog's claw scuffed along the street will pass
shiver on shiver down your spine again
like these nails scratching down your looking-glass.

And what would you ever do to change the line
your first sleep makes of eyelid into cheek
that you have never seen and I call mine?
This curl behind the ear that spoils your chic?

We are determined, love, for term of life,
and if we fold, it's blade into the knife.

Comfort

The slipping shoulder-strap – yet now with calm
I watch, and, yes, the old impatience still:
your thumb slips in, a neat barge of the arm
and comfort comes again; the slight cups fill
as hands pray backwards in a kid's quick drill:
naked you shiver in your ever green charm.
Such ingrained love of comfort in night's chill!
And then you leap in the dark without a qualm.

My comfort, you, whose comfort used to goad.
How do we do it? Arms in such a twist
all night. They'd cramp in moments if awake.
Sleepy, hoick my arm up over your waist.
Oh love, may such a comfort still hold good
the night your ghosts or mine begin to walk.

Present

This tiny squirrel ornament you chose
      to give me, knowing I love the miniature.
      You mean it for the smoky, bounding creature,
give me grace and lissomness, the fellow's
quizzical look. And, by some lucky chance,
      you have: they've slipped and made one darker pupil
      stare from the head, half-turned, as if the ill-
painted cone had caused him some perturbance.

You want to give all this. And I accept it.
      Cheeky fellow. Look, you couldn't guess
which hand he's in, so sleek and exquisite!
      Yet, love, it's only touches give such softness,
grace ... though hands, my hands that drowse your passive
shoulders feel more gentleness than they give.

Inklings

I came once on a place where a presence dwelt
that was no vestige of a living thing,
dank and foreboding, like a worldless suffering
condemned to leech into all life it felt;
the sudden brinking of a forest in the dark,
sheer on to silent waters, still as tar.
And now that place moves with me like a scar.

You plant your acorns, say we'll leave a mark.
– Love, let it be. The slant light clings to your hair.
The shadow of a flame, you block the sun.
What inkling of us would you nurture there
to brood upon the waters without form and void?
– You loop a twig and lift a sunset spun
into the trees. You blow. All ghosts destroyed.

Fledgling

That fledgling falls up fluttering to a bough.
I see an autumn leaf reverse, you say;
and spurt ahead – a child making a play
to catch it up, the street forgotten now.

– Oh, love, suppose the mind holds more than sense,
and things we love may bear some lasting trait
of us that later minds may mediate,
something survive where mind once grew intense.

You would return where roses are in bloom,
a concentration round a rose's scent;
or in the spring with swifts to skim and zoom,
and I shall not be there to watch you ache
to enter flower or flight.... Now, as you went,
you turn and breast the leaf-light, flake on flake.

Glimpses

Caught in the angle of the steps a shoe brad,
a crushed packet glinted; an ancient pool
of stagnant light wrinkled a tarmac roof.
An odd corner of the casual eye that had
Waterloo Bridge in mind, the pine-shaped, cool
scribbles of light. For days, like a reproof
too trivial to tell, that litter fixed my thought
with every glimpse of mine you'd never caught.

And one seen from a train: a Surrey field,
a split willow with fishing withes that leant
across a nettled ditch where pollen lay
denting the surface tension. So long concealed
and nothing much to tell: a moment spent
without you, love; the moments build away.

Her Prophecy

Three days after my death I shall return.
I will return and find you not in grief
but lost in quietude now past belief,
gazing upon the frost of patterned fern
across the panes ghosted with mist and trees.
You shall be calm as my oaks ridged with rime,
for all that you could not possess in time
has vanished – haven't I? – with ease.

For now you know there's nothing in the oaks,
nothing of me; there never was. I meant
those steady hands to cup a whorling bud
like life so tight they crushed it into scent.
Your world, that could not be to flesh and blood,
has vanished. Peace be with you – till it chokes.

Hearing the Flowers

There you go. Catch the minutest shudder
of petals in the fire's draught, and there you are,
your book a bird ruffling feathers in air
chilled by the sudden rustle of a shadow.

It frightens me, the mind, where it will shelter.
Sit beside me. Keats, in this fragment here,
more warm and capable to me, toward her,
than in his chosen works. Lean on my shoulder.

We're into words again. You're in my hands.
I'll hold the book for you. Murmur aloud
the living lines the dying hand still haunts;
your head weighs on my heart its mortal load.
You lose the place in shaking out your hair.
My love, it's far too close for flowers in here.

Duotone

Hands, hands to touch me like a sparrow's wings
gliding across a puddle's little sky.

> Gentleness, pressure, closer than murmurings,
> the flesh-tones pearling where my fingers lie.

Suavity, suavity of fingers, skim and plane;
husks of his touch I liquefy – I'm air.

> A shadow blown across a field of grain,
> the drifting of my hands along her hair.

In dream his touch is softer than the dark;
all moods, all modes of thought at the fingertips.

> What keeps such softness from my least remark,
> gentleness, pressure, speechless on my lips?

> Darkness we thought to enter with a torch.

Blind in the night we're dumb from talking touch.

Spectrum

My darling has the rain at her fingertips,
sun in her hair. Steady, she aims to make
a local little rainbow. Time, do not shake
though silver crescents swirl around eclipse,
as watching with wonderful patience here I stand,
considering where on earth the light will break,
coloured with some conviction for her sake.
Soon she will have me drinking from her hand.

You kneel and pick up grains of dust in the swirl
of several drops to make your spectral band.
Love, turn. I catch the spectrum in your hair,
and you, you easily could raise your hand,
arrange those drops of light on the odd curl
and take my word for rainbows in the air!

Clear Stream

The water runs through my fingers, always will.
Remember when I tried to drink from yours?
But you're away again, and the earth scores
your shadow on the run. I watch it spill,
the stain of water dark and shapeless. Hair
that flows like water as you chase or shake
it willowing down. Most taken with the air,
then most you're mine, though hardly for my sake.

Sooner or later you'll come back to cool.
The ground's too wet for anything so bare.
You'll find a way, a cat and water-shy.
How long we'll wait for shade to seep and pool.
Flow like water, my eyes caught in your hair,
our time turning.

Moth-Light

The sun-blaze sinks again and the brittle sky
shells over, yellow, luminescent green.
The light rusts through the black foil of trees,
and a martin zigzagzigs in a last flight.
Shadows, shadows, mindless shadows rise.
The countless times we've lazed till the last gleam
crumbles from the clouds, and it seems peace
we never came to come to us in time.

Your body says it is. Long shadows seep
to you and tide into small pools of shade.
I watch. I watch you watch. So many repeats
and nothing to speak of. The light that studs your eye
is light that glitters in a drop of rain.
Light of my eye, you moth-light to the mind.

Dusk

The years in the window pane, the daffodils
leaning stiffly like children's paper windmills
    still toward evening, the mitre buds of lilac.
    Wood-scent your hair was; young, your face looks back.

You start, shivering, at a boy's cry like God
along the street, and watch a girl go slipshod
    in her mother's high heels. Earliest starlight
    and you'd make out new patterns in the night.

And my hand, still dark to white on yours, though wizened.
    Enough now, was it ever enough to hold you,
this touch no words came close to in the end?

Love, leave the crazy tock of moth to window,
    the lamp light's cone an auburn head shines through.
Catch again the splendour of light in the wine-glow.

The Game

Now don't you fret. There is no other way.
Some time or other there must come an end.
What would you have? And how would it hurt less?
Come on, give me your hand, finish the game.
You'll see how softly I return its morse.
Then I shall get that good night's sleep
we never had those crazy times your sleek
shadow pranced and frescoed all four walls.

As I came out of darkness and found light,
and found it finer in your lively eye,
so into nothing I shall go and find
the cool moss of darkness was no lie.
I know where to turn. A starlit night;
take one of your walks now. I shan't mind.

Autumnal

Too close we breathe each other's tepid breath.
— The first time it was and meant to stick.
Late afternoon. A shoal of leaves windswept
across the window. You with your lousy gift
for drama: 'The leaves are falling, I must fly.'
Yet stayed to fling the window wide and catch
a leaf or two, then turned with a wet shine,
hair all over the place, one lacquered lash.

Autumn's hamming it up as ever again.
Odd angles like veins, the runnels down the pane.
A leaf with the rain's adhesion clings to the sill
against all gusts. My love, only last year
I willed that leaf to hold. The window chill
against my face, and your name coming clear.

The Oak

More shadow leaves than real on your old oak.
My touch more shadow than the day can clear.
Your face, a shade closer than the lure
of all the living; your body is the dark
beneath my hands. Was there ever light
enough for you? Was light ever enough?
Winter gave most. Now, love, you are the north
my memory steers from, late, so very late.

I cannot uproot an oak. I cannot move
the place I live, the mind derange its fix.
A few dead leaves lift on the aftermath.
We followed the foxgloves where the path forks;
it seems a way we never chose but took.
Now, love, I'm going down the other track.

Before Sleep

Barbaric ... yet I should have seen you dead,
and quelled the endless images of death
that rise up mouthing speechless from the depth
of time – your hand reaching again, condemned
to splay against a surface   tension stretched
like polythene. Your fingers whiten, press,
like children's noses, for rescue or to fend
me off. Oh make it clear. – There, on the breast,

a vein straggles like a silver birch.
Tell me it's not an image you intend.
Far love, I look with pity for the first
time ever on your body, feel a sense
of treason. It's finished, love. Leave off the frenzy.
We cannot even now be just good friends.

Revenant

My arm around you comforts me at night
that when the ghosts come you will not see,
nor the hooded Santa in the gown all white
and trimmed with blood. You would wake free

to clear my eyes, your body calm with sleep;
you, warmest, who were never much of a dream,
my arm around you.
                    – Or nights you creep back round
to me, your hazy gown our scheming wraith.

– My arm dragged in the dark across shroud white.
My blind spot in our room. Oh love, what's wrong?
You left my bed so many nights, one night.
Be reasonable, love; no, not the white lace.
Wear the quilted black. And don't be long;
my arm lays only a little warmth in your place.

Clearing

After so long to fetch up with silver birch,
bracken inflating with the breeze, the dry
springy mat of needles, the mind's purchase,
where only homely ghosts retrace the byways.

That trunk, with all the torsion of a girl
elbowing her slip above her head, dead wish
or memory. (A lifelong stepper-out, you were,
foot over silken splash with a cat's precision.)

No walks by still waters, hoping for seas,
nor where oaks writhe. These silver birch
will do; they always have, beyond all reason.
I shall not wander into you round here.
Winter is mine, the bare boughs emerging.
My ways have narrowed, these dry sticks my clearing.

Moth

A flake of wood, chip off the old block,
that's what you must be. And as for me,
I must be cracking up. Why otherwise
this inordinate affection for a moth,
the size of a fingernail? And on my clean
grey shirt. D'you think it's elm or pine?
D'you too seek refuge from the local woods?
The rust corrupts here. Tell me, what's the pull?

Flit. To the skirting-board. Why home on me?
Find yourself some bare and natural wood.
I won't clean too hard. I don't want to kill you.
Stay solo. More of you will pull the wool
over my eyes that way. No, out of that beam!
– Did she once wear a varnish of this colour?

Long Evenings

A patch of sun, you were, on the bare arm,
unnoticed by the mind in reading – warmth.
I read on in memory, for what it's worth,
to feel that sash of sun, and you not far.
The sunset moves around again. I stare
upon a page shone blank, till vision swims.
And long before, you would have come to whizz
the curtains to and shadow me and stay.

I turn the chair. A blade of iris spins
in a trill of its own local little winds.
Oh, love, I would have hastened up, long since,
to let you come and sit and see it twirl
from just this point of view. No, turn
your head a little more. No, as you were.

One Off

A cool glass, the long vista to the hill,
a girl, her shadow try-squared up the wall,
mirage of water on tarmac, glinting, still.
In the mind music I cannot quite recall.
And cherry blossom daisied on the grass.
A sun-shaft turns the pages of the book.
As once you held my eye, I watch her pass,
and someone waiting draws her with his look.

The movement, not the mover ... Oh, my love,
frivol of hesitation in the slow peal
of the skirt. (No, saffron yours, and blinding still.)
How many days that slight grace caught the life.
I could have buried all with that. ... To pull
off the time of our life in unrepeatable style.

Memorial

Not this see-through stuff of memory. Rock,
that's what I need, granite. No more black lace
like winter saplings linked across the sky.
– This saffron blurring. – Something I can knock
the roughness off for years and yet still trace
your fine features; something I cannot ply
with drinks – a slim throat I cannot choke –
Your mountain-force of hair in the sun-smoke.

Above the eyelash, single ply of cord!
Dove shadow in its curve; the arching brow –
who else saw that? strongbacked as a fish leaps.
How clear it is, and clean out of the mind's hoard.
How real ... love, is it you? Is it you now?
Let it be stone, love, where the flesh creeps.

Earth-Bound

Earth-flame, crocus under the ploughed bark,
earth-light, I have to kneel to look within.
Some peace, down here, horizon saucered, thin,
the children's noises scrambled through the park.
Half turn the head: blue sky without a mark
to move it by, though still that sense of spin.
Turn back, and let the mauving mist begin
before the sun makes everything go dark.

Earth-flame, earth-light – what kind of fool
would lay his head so close to rising fire,
so close to gnarling roots? Earth cool ... earth cool!
Low mist on the skyline, the chain-link wire.
So cool to touch, this bloom, a breath of air
stirring the steady flame to a small flare.

Window

Your eyes, child, in the window: the steady gaze
focused on nothing special, it would seem,
unless that chestnut in the day's last sun,
as though you wouldn't really dream of it
yet liked to think the candle's inner mist
would light the coming dark. Something of her
in that, her hidden self a wistful look.
More human yours and yet you stir dead love.

Reflections cross the pane but not your face,
and mine will never touch you as they pass;
my gangling matchstick man a trace of sun
no more to you across the grass. Yet, child,
your soft focus already blends out hers –
my love, you make the darkness personal.

from TOO MUCH OF WATER

DEDICATION

*For you who waste no speech
    to pass the light of day,
    contented with your mute
flowers, the natural pleach
    of boughs, I drop these lines.
Look, earth-spots in the snow
    where every grass-blade leans.*

Last Wishes

Love, sleep, and do not see me edge away.
    I cannot watch beside your death-bed.
Turn your head towards the close of day.
    I know the madness that is in your method.

How you will want the snowy impermanence of ash,
    your dust, like grass seed, flighted over heathland,
drifting in spinneys where the boughs clash,
    with matted needles laying waste beneath them.

Ah, settle on some narrower plot, beloved,
    among the blond spent grass and lie there;
not in the rain, nor in the wind ungoverned.
    Love, I cannot mourn you everywhere.

Last Words

All is as you have heard;
no, not asphodels,
not a gibbering word.

So you must think of rain;
on spring's first daffodils
I'll fall for you again.

But not for some years.
Last April's dust is laid
under a hollow lid.
And who is in these tears?

Spring

Yes, yes, we watched so many things die;
    lamented the fresh green of the willow
and sundry roses under this or that sky –
    and much else mourned into a pillow.

We knew full well it came to this.
    So I offer you this nostalgia of grief,
and these sprigs of forsythia, not much amiss,
    that blossom before they come to leaf.

Interflora

Ah, flowers … that said as much as your quick nudge
to snap a bee reversing, all velour;
your walks to calibrate a book of hours
with closures of your wild ones – all to scrap
your wristwatch half a year. I'll tell you flowers:
crocus slopped open like a pair of scissors
beyond the point of closing in the fist.
In my eye socket they incise their locus.

And since I cannot talk to you alive
I'll speak to you as dead, say it with flowers.
(More beauty in their day than in our life.)
They'll thrive, perfection's clones; nothing to me,
they'll pierce you with my nothingness – bleak
mauve footlings which you cannot pick and choose.

Byway

It's baffling, every time I pass, this shifty sense
that you had known the place, that we were intimates
of something here: a path; this now vestigial
track; which wild flower clump? what leafy fugitive
whose glimpse we'd make our own? But nothing tangible.

What is this? The lane is gone wherever it goes.
Never much of a one in my experience
for walks or views, why play the local genius
of diminutions? We never were unanimous;
what chance you'd keep omniscience to a picnic spot?

— I get you echoing, your voice a little wearier:
'Moments we had, the days, the days are vanishing.'

Look there! Lady's-slippers. Will they satisfy?
Let them. I'll track them down again. I promise you.

Rendezvous

You know: the old pear tree stood
beside the hazel. The evening gleam
hatched to silver the leaden stream.
— You will remember that spot
(I have taken pains you should)
whether you will or not,
with the coxcombs that you pull
from the cobnuts in the fall.
(Come back, Peter; come back, Paul.)

Where it used to shrink or fill
only a row of hazel sprigs.
And it dried out in my time.
— The name of that bourn is Styx,
poor, bare, forked, divining stem.

Word

No, don't you question, not for a split second,
how straight to you my love has been — or will be.
The likes of you, soft-centred and unrationed,
can't know what I betray to leave you easy.

One comfort I will give you. It must answer.
So right you are. You never held me clearly.
I made a vow because I can't do other
and honour it I will until it croaks me.

Owl-flight and word hold straight through darkness.
Shadow of flame, whose love is love truly?
Our vows, our trusts, to stay the world process:
and these words, love, shall they outlast our story?

Clusters

That many must have loved in this grey world
much as we have is some companionship
as once again I trace the languid sweep
your brow-bone makes, wing of a frigate bird.
I tell myself that I can love the years
that fanfold from the corner of your eyes,
your laughter; more, how I alone can phase
the shadowed hint of dove your lids curve clear.

Even the galaxies cluster deep in space;
infinitudes of planets where we lie
again together linked in love or sleep.
– Ah, my love, it's unbearable society.
Even this desperation, that steers my hand
to grip you, grips you also in the stars.

Moment

If you could know how much I train myself
against that moment you would understand
my quiet anger at your breakneck paths,
your bare legs angled in the sun like fish;
my vacant gaze on you patient in the flowers,
hidden in sprays of bright forsythia,

the stems unseen, your time-drift galaxy.
In so much green to gloss the turn of day!

And you might gather then, even in dream,
how in my restlessness I turn to you
and touch that lath of muscle by your ear
and stir a tress because I cannot bear
to watch you sleep away when I have thought
to keep all for myself the darkest night.

The Brooch

It's not so much the amber stone.
    I don't think any follow quite,
but you perhaps will get the gist:
    I bought this filigree on sight
because it seemed to catch the tone
    of silver birch in silver mist.

The gift, not giving, is the gist;
    but why I love that tone in tone
I can't get clear, nor really quite
    why you should ever like the sight
of silver birch more than the stone.
    You'll please me if you wear the mist.

Over that rise we'll find low mist
    and find the birch but not your stone.
Come from behind me, hand in glove.
    Primeval instincts still persist:
I almost turned on you. Oh love,
    the cracking twig bred in the bone.

Path

Now we have come to this. Take a long look.
After the years, the wandering, this the return:
the landscape, if you say, of childhood. – Fern,
we couldn't see beyond it. Never that brook
you try unravelling to the sky's scuffed brink,
the caterpillar hedgerows wandering far.
This path, and beechnuts we were hunting for.
Our matchstick shadows buckled down and shrank.

I cannot bring myself to shuck them now;
I feel the tricorne husk lifting the nail.
But we'll be back and often now you know. –
Beechnuts. My stylish love, you'd have to kneel.
Listen, grasshoppers chirring in the quitch
like the spasmodic winding of a watch.

Wall

Oh not again. Two hundred miles from home
the tile-topped wall, pointed with angled moss,
an ancient puddle in the rutted loam,
fly-wings of oil. And was it? Yes, it was,
loosestrife. – A moment seen those years ago
one everlasting country afternoon.
Ah, now the dust and heat and thirst of June,
and, worse, an echo of that wretched hope:

that there would be in time a postern gate,
and gnats, loyal as these eye-motes, gone;
and we should come upon a shaded lawn,
not as expected guests or the long lost
but visitants of joy, and glimpse at last
the past intrinsic flit like a rabbit's scut.

Exorcism

You're boning up on me again. The years
I've waited! Hardly. More like stopped and paused
in odd moments, hearing some phrase once yours,
for you to sidle up – and dither-paced
as usual. I know. I know all your shifts:
limp jokes – you couldn't stand a decent silence;
fidgets you took for action or resilience;
fake laughter turning jester all my shafts.

You never had the nerve to lie quite straight.
Palters and shifts. Now it all must wait.
Or can you fidget up some haze all white;
or shall I come to get you? Fat chance, it seems.
You're getting warm. Warmer. ... Only in dreams
the living haunt the dead in their long night.

Gifts

Upon the flyleaf your dearest name
      and: Happy Christmas, Nineteen Eighty;
      a book you'll toss aside so lightly,
thinking it dull, as may be I am.

One day you'll read and love this volume,
      as well I knew when I inscribed,
      and, seeing the diminutive script,
you'll wish perhaps it were on vellum.

And bridge to these old days behind
      as once I did, discarding a hymnal
      and catching in it like a hangnail,
on the endpaper my father's hand.

Against Superstition

FOR DONALD DAVIE

Most vows sworn in youth long broken;
attrition of years yawns rightly so;
but one sworn deep and never spoken,
made to myself those rigid years ago.

Never to write a congratulatory line,
never to fellow maker speak in verse,
for to speak so would twice assign
the poet's title – from all but Death a curse.

Thus, as Landor, who is safely dead,
I now address you, in this guise
risking Death's silence on my head,
and you who taught me much say is it wise?

Winters

IN MEMORIAM YVOR WINTERS

Because you knew how all earth's furies
    could leak through candle-flame into a room
you latched on reason's mail against the lurid
    and caught the light but not the gloom.

And since you thought the evil of the curse
    could only be removed by words that wove
no spell by feeling's fluke or mind's inertia,
    proof in themselves though in the sacred grove,

I shape these words, the almost foreign parlance
    we both imagine ours as born and bred,
and weave your myth of reason against all jargons,
    here in this study lit by nuclear dread.

Birds

FOR KEVIN CROSSLEY-HOLLAND

Not the opinions and propositions of Livy,
Cicero's studied rhetoric, Virgil's stately rhythms –
this dead lingo of squared stones, more gaudy and more lively,
naive flowers and gawky birds, the dolphin-rider's,
in frieze and mosaic, uncluttered and lovely.

Full sun helps to envisage them, lax on their hillside –
none of the Lachrimae Christi, more proto-Frascati.
Never before inveigled by sun, I people the whole scene,
envy their space, this same light with the high cloud scudding,
though they stroll in my head as I sit on the hall seat.

Yet my flier is none of their stiff-legged, perky songsters;
no, nor car-crushed sparrows killed in their hedge-hopping:
the lone hawk that held its glide through the gable's sawn trees,
down the banquet-hall, above the mead and the harping,
out into darkness with the smoke ascending.

Fishbourne

An Apology

FOR ROBERT LOWELL

A touch of jealousy, good shade,
it must have been when I deplored
the second thoughts you spread abroad,
your chance to change what you had made.

The printed phrase you could reword
in answer to the wayward muse;
so let the rashness of my views
be never seen again or heard.

Considered long, too late expressed,
I breathe this brief apology
and covet with keener jealousy
your incommunicado rest.

The pathless search that hoodwinked you
has led me through the mud and mire
where all that comes of mortal fire
is jack o' lanterns half seen through.

Rest, rest, immortal spirit, rest
upon your laurels once again
and leave me to the itching pen
where straight deletion's much the best.

Summer Shadows

That toddler, hoicking his shadow bootee up the step,
like someone who has stuck his foot in tar,
will make in later time a summer of this spell.
    His mother, laughing at the top,
her hair in tints of copper beech may store
for someone summer in a lock that will not pale.
I watch the roadstone in the tarmac form and speed
like comets through my shadow, raise my pace
    to see them hasten – which has spurred
a boy with whirr of tyres to race and pass.
Quicksilver threads, light vacillates along each spoke.
    And there beyond the brow expands
        in my mind, at least,
after the tunnel of trees, like green arrested smoke,
the everlasting sea on ever lengthening sands.
    Cease! Ceased.

Ah, woman, child, and man and boy, unknown confrères,
your shadows, briefer than a roadside rose,
hold still, imprinted as one summer's phase,
    glossed forms through which no stone careers.
No chiaroscuro of leaves obscure this frieze!
Loved silhouettes, whose darkness time intensifies,
I'd give you names; I'd conjure namesakes with your image,
and times to come recall this choice of summers
    fading to the future's, homage
of eyes that look upon these gleams and shimmers.
Yet, if they come to love them, no second sight,
    but poignant with what's dead and done –
        as in their day.
Ah, love, you're somewhere in this summer's light,
walking the wild flower paths, out of the sun,
    away, away.

Contingencies I'd fix in frescoes made of slate.
Shadows of flame cast out by greater light,
I cannot let you go where all the leaves are strewn,
    a summer sepia obsolete.
I'd give you by some quirk or sleight
indelible salience. – First drops of rain
tacked into the pavement, that avenue
of flowering cherry's earliest pinkest snows –
    Cobham.... It's all together now.
Once, once, but where I can no longer recognize....
Unknown comrades, I've spoken for your sakes and mine.
    In asphalt pavements, a decor of flakes.
        But what will hold
together is a redolence returning, touched with brine....
Love, comb, comb out the rain-fresh scent of woods and brakes....
    The shades turn cold.

from EARTH LIGHT

Portents

Strangest things have happened before,
    again, and mostly elsewhere:
sparrows will nest in a tractor – folklore
    the runes of geese on the air.

And our recounting them as rare
    bandies their wonder back to us ...
and if the thrush we see is a fieldfare
    is the marvellous instance bogus?

And if, love, we both speak at once
    in the light of some other summer,
and say it is love, in all conscience,
    it has happened again somewhere.

Our shadows link hands in the wild flowers,
    gangling their length on the pathway,
and that chink-chink we hear as ours
    lights only once on this twayblade.

Cranesbill

Delicate misty bloom
    huddled away like your words,
a cranesbill of powdery blue,
    mute for all its worth;

not to be gathered or pressed
    where it may grow again.
Let it grow here for the present
    we never took nor gave.

Gifts

The thoughts I have I cannot give.
I hardly bear them well myself.
Gifts of my hands I'd like to give
and tell we share them here and now.

What the gift gives is what I'd give –
behind this dumb, so yellow bloom.
I'd like to give you happiness,
the cat that seldom comes when called.

Occasions

I wasn't there to look
      the time you saw the lightning sear
the crooked oak.
      I had your fear for it.

I wasn't there the day
      you found a windcast blossom-shadow
spread from the may.
      Your joy I had for that.

– You let the bird go free.
      I couldn't see the hope that welled
but it seemed to me
      a bulb you held had bloomed.

When the love that I swear
      is a dry husk on the wind's breath,
I shan't be there.
      You'll have my death for it.

Willow Walk

Willows cascade their curtains
over the towpath, into the water.
My legs go torpid; I cannot enter
    that tunnel.

The way you threw your tresses
over your forehead, into the basin,
your hands flurried, the trickles coursing
    the spine's runnel.

The blinking of an eyelid,
the shutter's action; there, at the outlet,
time, the axeman, with his mindless
    blade of light.

Memento

What is this, you can't remember?
You have it pat if I forget.
You gave your word. The sun was amber,
setting. You know, by that gate.

So low it silvered drops of rain
beneath the bars. You reached your right
hand out to them, your fingers ran
them through and cross-marked the straight.

It's unbearable you can't remember.
The world's tears, woman. I was there.
That cliff of cloud, bruise-black and sombre
above the sunset's orange shore.

Some game! Forget the promise, love.
Recall the place that you swore on.
Yes, circumstantial – known as life.
We cannot go back there again.

Trapezoid shadow of the gate –
We used to try to change each other.
I can't believe that you'd forget.
When was it that we gave it over?

Violets

Oh, yes, you brought the violets in,
on to the kitchen sill,
to save them from the winter,
poor mangy things.

You and your green fingers.
But I know the drill.
You'll tell them, every spare minute,
of the summer they missed.

Another I never let you have.
And they will parrot it back,
your smattering of a purple patch.
Flowers respond to chat.

Everyone's heard of that.
You've certainly got the knack.
What a summer we will have,
these winter annuals.

Antique

A silver candelabra, love?
Why on earth a candelabra?
Silver? Never in your life!

Or is it the olden days you're after:
a bit of tallow in an old tin?
Which of whose forebears lit a castle?

The twisted stems at every turn
reflect a tilted flame of lamp light
a marriage of convenience, and tone!

But we can never light those candles;
Could we get back to last spring, love?
You leapt from my grasp, darted to paddle

your hands in the bluebells' haze, and the life
came back to you in that wild laughter,
at finding a pool the storm had left.

I've waited for you in the thick of darkness,
well-shaft to a pitch lid of water,
my head obstructing the only star-point.

Do not come back, my bluebell wader,
do not pull back from your dwindling pool.
Once in living memory your wood.

Look, I have lit the candles. They pile
our quaking shadows over us.
Watch them. Watch as their tears spill.

Goldenrod

More is forgotten than remembered.
    I cannot tell you why it is I hate
       these goldenrod. I've always hated them,
and any goldenrod, by any gateway.
    One day when I am old and the glossed light
       of childhood seems eternity too late,
it may come back to me in living spite,
       prompting some feeling for an hour or spasm –
       dull, yellow-dusted peaks of even height –
when, deaf to me, the feigned enthusiasm
       of your vague words that never had a season
       is painless as passing time, the trembling aspen;

and love's become as trivial as these
        stalks of goldenrod, well out of it,
        that I smash and enjoy smashing as I please
because they have their season, and they split
        cleanly, unlike the pliancy of trees.
– Now match your forceful mouth to this mad fit.

Bric-a-Brac

The glance of years ago,
        one forgotten afternoon,
you cannot now return, eyes slow,
        the gaze immune.

Okay, look around the room,
        old gifts, odd curios shelved;
silent, uninvolved, presume –
        your years undelved.

Clairvoyant to my days,
        you have the vantage over me.
Date my ivory, appraise
        this fake in memory:

a naked figurine, its style
        wide open, one for a pair,
Chelsea blue period, trial
        piece, none too rare.

Come in, do; and ring the bell,
        eyes immune, slow as that swan
in all-time junk. Pawn and sell,
        the antique con.

Mirrors

The best and worst of us
      catch ourselves in a pose.
There, sprinting for a bus,
      already off the pace,
to some more sporting era –
or true self in the mirror?

The baton raised to beat
      with hair and zip and flair;
the record turns, a sweet
      plush hush on the floor
of some melodious era –
or true self in the mirror?

Caught in the lamp-lit room
      beyond the window pane,
the scholar who'll exhume
      the classic long-lost paean
of some more noble era –
or true self in the mirror?

Neat harp of the shoulder-blade,
      adze-scoop down the neck,
Eve, is it?, now portrayed,
      and naked as her nook
in that most perfect area –
or true self in the mirror?

Ah, barest one, is it you,
      self-mirror, self-admirer?
At other times are you true?
      Is paradise your era?
Or, *Mirror and the Sylph*,
you're naked as yourself?

LIKE A VOW

Local Colour

It feels like farewell to leave this area,
as if to go would lose some thing of value,
though what it is I have no clear idea.

Not those cool harmonies, ochre and blue,
these hessians, barley golds, the rusting bracken,
the Autumn scorches in the fields of fescue.

That path, its track of single wheel-ruts, then;
redolent of somewhere that it wanders,
some journey long to rest, some friend forgotten?

No ... nor the angled bough whose shadow stirs
some element of dream across the moment.
Nothing to do with you, my love, nor others.

It holds no aura of a lost event,
mine or the land's; no calm of mind; no trespass;
nor is there terror in it like a portent.

It's almost love that holds me to this space –
despite a world I thought to leave at will –
in dread its power may rise in other places.

Recapitulation

A blade of cold water down the throat:
huddle of trees and shrubs like green sheep;
the mill-pond brimming still as lead with threat.

And, if, with these unsummoned into shape,
they all are there, and bound up with my head,
all days are there to rise with detail sharp,

can't I riffle to whichever day I had,
and won't one show me what it is I want –
untouchable, exact, and facet-hard,

as once I stared myself into a squint
to catch, in the spouting barley-sugar-amber,
the skelter of the tea-leaves as they went?

Nothing. But in the cup the usual number,
dregs, always dregs – though grandmother at least
made fortunes of them, as I now remember

one distant day when I was fearfully lost –
wrong fork across the heath, not seen ahead,
when coming from her cottage – time now glassed,

untouchable, enacted, period.
And what the child would not, cannot know:
speedwell, red campion, in all likelihood.

– So many lanes they waymark and renew
that lead to nothing much that I would find:
speedwell, red campion, ragwort, I name them now.

They intervene, again have intervened,
but those days passed as weeds some mood or itch
idly dispersed, or swinging jacket fanned.

Day! Where is the day I did not watch
hands move, mind churn – its laughter free or feigned?
Merciless eye, that nothing can assuage!

Upland

I

A dry ditch, with banks of leaf-mould
like wet rust, chestnuts overhanging;
a slate sky, contoured with sun-gold

above the horizon where a hamlet
glistens. There will be rain, rain falling
big and warm and straight as a plummet,

splashing up coronets.... Forgotten
the hamlet's name, the last turning,
which next, but southern the location.

But I was on that upland; remember
a pressure binding and releasing.
My memory haunts it like a spectre.

Perhaps it is the mind of others
that leaguer there almost a feeling.
– You would assume the wild-eyed watchers.

I find you many likely places.
But if you're there you show no inkling.
You give them all your keenest glances,

then off into the woods to savour
the bluebells' well attested pooling –
lady's-slippers found one summer.

But what is missing I cannot capture
in trees, lane, ditch, the cloud purpling.
It is nothing that is in your nature.

But I am nearest it in silence:
the sound of a bell no longer ringing.
It's almost like an old allegiance,

fealty sworn young to a lost lord.
You cannot swear faith to my ghost-king.
I cannot breach his word, his gold-hoard.

Your bluebells, lass, this is your kingdom.
In my lord's realm I'm the hireling.
Kneel to the bluebells, the blown blossom.

No once and future king, forespoken:
his line will never see returning.
My oath can never be forsaken.

2

Lord, in the underlight of thunder –
But if my liege is self-projection,
no ghostly exile of a lost order,

loyalty is no less, though kingship
is mine. What worse than king's treason?
I can't break faith by cant or gossip.

I say: no feint of trees and shadow.
Not mine but earthly the dominion;
the bond is real as voice and echo.

No: beeches these; the promised shower
small rain; and the wide sky ocean-
grey, not true to scarp and tenor.

But let it be: a part and parcel,
our common ground of recollection,
the great, down-sweeping branches focal.

(Curled husks of nuts like Dutch bonnets,
the shortcut – geese in opposition,
a slate sky harrying high cloudlets.

We used to eat the nuts when children,
nails lifted by the shell's construction.)
Childhood, and the big rain not fallen.

    3

Coronets of rain – and the keen-eyed
child recalls their brief existence,
sprung from the tarmac of the roadside.

And, going up the narrow staircase,
Candleman prancing like a nuisance,
coronets, tumbled in a goose chase,

rolling down the gleaming roof-tops....
In the stillness of leaves and birds, the silence,
the weathered spirit senses raindrops,

knows the freshness that falls, releasing
the tension, bringing out the fragrance
of the grass, the dry ditch jingling.

– Trembler of light on its white column,
coronets tumbling, dancing attendance,
Candleman, Candleman, once his kingdom. –

But to your beeches as I know them,
my scarp, how shall we plot our credence?
To know another takes a kingdom.

And the big rain is falling, watcher,
the big drops in their regular cadence,
bigger than any tears, and warmer.

The Sunken Path

A land it was without companion.
No feature to detain the eye,
no sign of human cultivation.

I do not know how many times
I'd been there; have no recollection
of what event, nor where or why.

And yet it will not be forgotten:
the grass banks burred first left, then right,
like hammered pegs, the path so sunken

Those weird birches, trunks awry,
the course that raindrops latch on
down a dirty pane – and the pines,

encroaching pines at the edge of vision.
The path wound up a steepish climb,
toward a slate sky without motion.

– Years ago, years, the lingering sight,
but clearer, sharper the depiction.
It seems to lock into the mind.

*

But what holds over the hill-crest?
Do the pines' serrations meet
like jaws – a dark aquarial forest?

Was shelter once the driving need,
from bead-curtains of rain – or coolest
shade from the dusty August heat?

The path draws upward, still the clearest.
If you'd been walking there with me,
there would be something you had noticed,

a skipper, wild flower prove it real.
Your eye for small things always honest
to pin locality on a dream.

Show me the colour of bugloss, dearest;
fix it as somewhere you have been,
you with your eye for a wren's nest.

   *

But which and where are the companions?
Are they long-barrowed by the tread;
this the landscape of extinctions?

– In mind, I climb the likely bed
of winter rills, and the desertions
grow as congenial as a friend.

The path holds no commemorations.
Nor were you one to reach the head.
The air trembles with the derelictions.

There should be, just beyond the crest,
a church of leaning headstones, apparitions
of other people's, not my dead,

living times out of mind, deletions
of lichen, moss, the rain's fret;
but I, too, have made my exactions.

I have buried them before their death;
the living shall not haunt their perditions.
Love, the landscape seeps into my head.

   *

– The boy stares long into the window,
watching a raindrop dither downward,
seeing another and another follow.

They're lit to silver at an awkward
juncture, to silver birch; the narrow
path meandering, pine bordered.

– Wenceslas footsteps, huge and hollow,
stilting the loose sand, striding upward,
those crumbling edges of sand-grains harrow

with the erratic stealth of rivered
drops on the pane that make an ox-bow
but always edging, inching earthward.

– The horror of bubbles on the cocoa
bursting, the dry grains uncovered,
imprinting memory like a furrow.

*

Where are the friends of this madness?
Banish me from the lie of this land.
Love, show me the colour of bugloss.

Gesture

Sand not discernible from sea,
the sea not separable from sky,
mist like eroding promontory.

A girl zigzags the shingle, striding
that drives her flaring yellow skirt
against her thighs, like flame plying

from underneath a bough; exertion
flapping her blonde hair from her shoulders –
a gale of her own with each diversion,

veering till mist obscures, then strolling
clear a moment. She has no plan,
no firm direction that is holding.

– Blurring the foreland, rifted in canyons,
encroaching combers that churn the stones –
mist and sea are her companions.

    *

That self-wind, mine. She plays the loner:
hair and skirt, haphazard walk,
her pleasure in themselves, and donor

of mine, the emblems of a haughty
sorrow, germane to mist and headland,
consoled by sea, the wave's exhaustion.

And to the life! It is the death
of hope. (Long live hope, the skirt knows;
long live hope, the blonde hair threshes.)

Pensive, perhaps, a child, she notes
the sand responding to her feet,
like skin beneath some grip or load.

And so it may be joy, the freedom
of lonely cove and lingering mist,
nonchalant gestures; none to read them.

    *

Mist and darkness obscure the figure.
A year ago? The gestures bloom
in streets and crowds, indelible vigour;

on hoardings, film – a casual beauty
or routine, but as the leaf runs true,
sorrow or joy, allusion, illusion.

– Six feet of light between us, and soon the
dark. I want to reach my hand
to touch your hand. It is the movement

of twenty years ago, this angle,
wandering like a stopped clock in time.
Love? It is the gesture. The candle

has not changed its spear of light;
my gnarled hand knows its root and branch.
A thousand shearwaters, one dive.

The Hill

IN MEMORIAM R. C. GRAY

I cannot do anything with this landscape,
while you have settled down to see the views,
and gaze across the valley to some mansion

sinking in green suds of trees – amusement
enlivened for a moment by a train,
scaled to a model, that you find a nuisance.

I'd rather have it animate the ancient
peace, I suppose it is, of field and covert;
but no hand will descend on it – extraneous –

and shift it to some tunnel. I have no love
of miniatures, no god's yen for omniscience.
The aftermath is cut and stacked and covered.

And the path leads to stepping-stones; listen:
the sluice of water that is water. Tears
would sound the same in volumes such as this.

There is no voice in the stream's whispered hearsay.
There is no beauty here. It's all my eye.
See with the moth's light; catch the talon's fierceness.

Our tread erodes the path like the rain lying
on the sun's scorched earth; soft or wild, the rain
that I'm attuned to more than any shining

of the sun – rain never visited with angels.
And I remember once a day of downpours
when Bob, my friend – dead, in his strength, of brain-stroke –

spread one oilskin upon the grass and, pounded
by thunderous drops, both huddled, makeshift-tented
under the other cape against the trouncing.

We had a grass-furred oilskin when it ended,
and months before we'd plucked each blade or strand;
a talking point for years, our launching sentence.

My eyes are locked through rain into this landscape,
the stream and stepping-stones, the lucid shallows,
for my dead friend, and all of those whose handwork

is buried in each feature of the valley.
Love, you shouldn't see it from this angle.

Hold still. A leaf's caught in your hair. Mallow?

River

To hold in mind
these twisting paths,
this peace like the river winding.

How long will either keep
unblurred such peace
to flow on, sinewed, leaping?

That wren to be your emblem,
its jiffy poise,
pole-vaulter bending its stem?

Or these few speedwell mine
to make us pause,
return the river's winding?

But years, in distant years,
this time of peace
a drifting branch of hearsay?

That wren toppling a stem,
the speedwells' place?
Or like a vow remembered?

* * *

The Water-Splash

The water-splash, you called it,
typical understatement.
A long time since I saw it.

But still in mind located
and you still on the high point,
gazing long to savour it.

Dumb appreciation. Silence…
We knew we'd change, and thought
this, too, would be sanitized.

Our focal waterfall,
like an old English sheepdog
lolloping nowhere forwards.

He has no name or meaning,
but I have sent you this dog,
summers, as if you'd see it.

No telepathic responses;
your clear eye unflummoxed:
water and stone and mosses.

You and the falls a comfort,
while I have lost the place,
imagined every summer.

And on a heat-hazed day
I picture you on the slope,
and see the dog again.

Fetch him, boy! Fetch him home!
(Shoo him off and dismiss him
or you'll be soaked all over.)

I can't understand this distance.
How was it less than your death?
I'm not used to the difference.

And back comes old tousle-head
every summer into mind;
and the water-splash, as you had it.

Still

Daughter, you are – if photograph
     may tell the truth without the eyes
    touching in shady velleities –
your grandmother's image and proof.

As was your mother – with the same if.
     From those old days: the untrammelled gaze;
    such carefreeness that never goes;
the lace but useless handkerchief.

– Speedwell after speedwell, path
     or hedge to tell each by her place
    and time, the trellises, the plush,
a future like a picnic heath.

It's more than mood, the hasty comb,
     blouse loose, unceremonious.
    I cannot swear to carefreeness,
but hope you may, in time to come.

Not as a grey nostalgiast
     but knowing what had been yourself.
    – Lass, must the held frame dissolve?
Both hold the present in the past?

Speed well, my only lass, speed well!

Sun

Dave, you were early dead
and, silly bugger, asked for it,
I'm afraid it must be said,
the way you drove. You must admit
it was the one thing you could do
to reconcile the world to you.

On this marvellous summer day
I remember you – not with tears,
affection, or regret I must say,
but pleased that after nine years
even with sods of your cut and run
death itself has not quite won.

Correspondences

Letters as frequent as English rain,
    you have kept faith for twenty years,
    and faithfully that face appears
in mind, that shock of hair like grain
    before the scythe.

Don't tell me: you made the pub seethe
    hearing your plot to roast a swan.
    I now expect that marathon,
your six-mile trek in the blizzard's teeth
    to meet – by air.

Leaves under the closed door are
    lost voices in a foreign tongue.
    We scuffed them all about when young.
I've swept them up each year so far
    without fail.

Fall or Autumn, Autumn and Fall.
        And these rose-petals I gather
           make a wine that will not travel,
a scent and flavour I cannot file
        like an old address.

File this then in your legendries:
        this photo of a grey-haired idler
           (that doesn't really travel, either)
daydreaming into the autumn trees,
        willows and wyches.

And what you cannot see he watches:
        indolent swans on quiet waters,
           cupping, like hands, wings poised and faultless
to catch the light; and his half-wishes
        for that candid white.

Communication

FOR IAN HAMILTON

Now miles and years have intervened,
do you, as I do yours, old friend,
still read my books? Would either read
them more if one of us were dead?
        And would a voice unearthed recall
        the years of silence that appal?

Souvenir

The very earth on which they stood
        is gone, three fists of withes,
poor pollards tilted at the wood's edge,
        reeds like scythes upended, crossed.

Beneath cloud slabbed with storm,
    their image skimmed with light.
Far friend, I hope with you a faded torment.
    Hindsight seems the last betrayal.

Life-Lines

Reading, in your hand, the searing care:
a lifelong friend insane, a child dead,
the bonds of love that tear, I catch the pain
in all you wrote and said.

I leech into your sorrow again – forgive me,
feeling through all I read in your slant black.
In the dead season I live, old friend, I need
even this to clutch me back.

The Lost Ones

'Thy speech bewrayeth thee ...'
    – ST MATTHEW, 26.73

The little girl had died at night.
I read the column in morning sun,
and two days since the crime was done;
I ought to take up pen and write.

(The mother never read a line,
the culprits never read a verse,
no reader mourned behind the hearse;
what critics came to seek a sign?)

Little ones have died last night
in Bangladesh and Birmingham,
Morocco, Chad and Vietnam,
and all parts out of mind and sight.

(It would be honester by far
bewraying lilies of the field –
where they grow is bone-mealed, bone-mealed –
our little pretty ones they are.)

More little ones will die tonight.
Little ones die by Christ and Zen
and no blood runs from any pen.

And this is all I wrote tonight.

Steps

(*A woman is speaking*)

Ah, let him count my footsteps down the street!
As if he could, this quiet night of snow.
But only these two feet go down the flags
and back again – wet pewter in the white.

I should have walked the unmarked roofs instead!
Daisies they look like, all those scrambled stars.
Soundlessly I tread; I'm like the snow.
This snow will never tell me who I am.

No tally of my footsteps in this hush.
Tonight, I'll pad up barefoot, soundlessly.
Back of a scrubbing brush, this dusty sole.
Strange with what narrowness we hold the ground!

A Woman Speaks to God the Father

Lord of the entire universe,
was there no one else to take?
No lively son in the womb's hearse,
no supple girl for you to break?

But you must take my dolphin man?
No boy to fall to you in play,
no white head broken like a fan,
no sinewed arm for you to fray?

Must I be jealous all my life
of six feet of claggy earth;
jealous of every trotting wife,
of every brat that's given birth?

I am jealous of you, God.
If I had every inch your might,
in my black hole you'd spoil your rod;
you'd kick up stars in endless night.

Homage to Robinson Jeffers

You chose the bed by the sea window
        for a good deathbed
when you built the house. You had it waiting,
letting only the odd guest sleep there,
not knowing its purpose,
yourself perhaps amused, as Death with you.

I don't know whether you died
        in that bed by the sea window.
I hope you did. It is a small right,
like a birthright, the deathright
that we have betrayed like so much else
in this canned world that clutters the sea-rocks.

Your room that I have never seen
        I have always imagined,
rock-clean, relentless as your rhythm,
clear with dawnlight or the storm light,
noise of the great sea crashing beyond.
How I envy that clarity.

Wherever I reach my end, Jeffers,
          it will be in that sea room.
You whose words live on
have given me, unlike the Christ,
a place to die.

Memorial

FOR FRANCES HOROVITZ

I never met you.
      The gut reaction
to mourn your death is
      driven by anger
that time should wreck not
you as yourself but
as anyone else so
      circled with love,
      gentle with life.

Nothing I miss is
      you or yours to
wrench recognition.
      I cannot mourn you.
I'd have to give you
characteristics,
a touch, some charisma
      of others I love to
      feel your destruction.

Eleanor's hands,
      cool even in summer –
the image happens
      with such a sudden
shudder of anguish
and terror I am so
cold that I cannot
      touch myself. My
      hands mourn your death.

MIRRORS, WINDOWS

(*A soliloquy: a middle-aged man observes his dead father's features in his reflection in the window pane*)

A Likeness Reflects

Look at it, old face, in the window pane.
What do you think it feels? Thought you once knew:
timidity disguised beneath long patience;

weak humour an evasion playing neutral;
that everlasting hustle to escape
from any issue, household, local, nuclear?

– Tousled hairstyle, the voice's measured cadence,
those heavy spectacles ... they hardly hide
the likeness. How have you come up to occasion?

But then it wasn't yours. (Who else with the hindsight?)
– You don't have to sit here and face this carping.
There you are, let that squirrel take the high jump!

(Too many mirrors.) Spiral the trunk, scarper,
forelegs wide, back humped, a grand prix car.

The Garden Beyond

A steady wind flows through the cherry tree;
along the topmost twigs aligns the leaves
like minnows swimming, motionless, upstream.

That low plank bridge across the bourn, a legion
of tiddlers holding station underneath;
those planks an ankle-width apart, unleashing

fears of legs in traps, a dread of kneeling
with all the rest. – Laughter without amnesty.
(Look away, face; true mirrors are amnesiac!)

Fear of water so deep it reaches to tears.
That inching down the face like insect duos.
– Dream of the leg bleeding ants, ants teeming.

Open the door. The rain will have to do
for this, child. Out. Out. Open the door.

Reflection Answers Back

The bonehouse has no doors, and all the windows
reflect the images of self-defeat,
self-aggrandisement and self-acquittal.

Sit still. We'll flesh each other out, feature
for feature. Look on me, old man; as you used
to look; look on your son, feeling for feeling.

The long wait for triumph is over for you.
Not that gaze again, tacit and fixed.
You haunt weaker dead than living on my youth.

Silence consent? Or dumb déjà view? Fidget,
go on, give no answer. But do something.
Play with your pens, you've a whole fistful.

Old man, look on him; look on your son
with that shiftless iron stare, that air presumptive.

Reflection Rebukes and Challenges

There is a time for speech, a time for silence.
Death gives most men but you the sense of it.
There was a time for words; you did not desire them.

What the headstone speaks the living issue.
The dead shall not come to living beck and call.
You never heard me speak, not a single instance.

Ventriloquize me now from your little corner.
Speak to your son. (The pane stares back at you.)
Your son, not me. Time for the wise and cautious.

Ventriloquize me now! Here's to reunion!
And I shall tell if you talk in character.
I shall reflect on his and your ill-usage.

Ventriloquize me: muggins, the taciturn.
(Who says does not know. But you're determined.)

The Garden Beyond and Beyond

The minnow leaves have made no sign of headway,
flickering like light tethered in the current.
– What water, sprats of sun, when Bob, quite helpless,

flashed skidding through the ford, one dry escutcheon
where saddle shielded trousers!
                                      A sort of shining.
Like couch-grass heads the gutter ripples scurry.

– The gold nib gleamed and buckled with my shying.
It was that day of grief my mother died.
I watch it crumple. Sorrow? Selfish icon,

my first fountain-pen, or true digraph?
Under the table with the torch-light dimming,
waiting for dark to hone the beam, motes diving

and soaring in the shaft. – I watch them dither,
drifting out into night. (Moth, you are dizzy.)

Wise and Cautious

Son, I cannot tell you how to live.
The lightning lasts a flashy second's worth.
Rock can't keep the spate inside its limits.

Oak cracks in storm; but mouths may keep their word.
I promise nothing; we shall miscomprehend
each other and possibly do much worse.

Yet do not look on this in long years hence
and blame yourself for every misconception,
nor grieve when I am gone upon this head.

Promise me nothing; vows are sworn to the self:
make sure the word you give will wear like diamond.
(And one other thing: get yourself an obsession!)

Son, I cannot tell you how to die.
So do not watch me. No date for your diary.

Reflection Heckles

That's not very knowing. What do you say?

My words are silent. Silence that is golden.
(Slaves of the crucified deserve the same

in image of the only (mis)begotten.
You couldn't manage that, so had to sham
self-martyrdom, all those petty golgothas.)

Not even the sun is enough. We are shadows
of flames and risk becoming the shadows of bombs.
Twice a day the brilliant sun can shackle

our hindleg stance to its stalking bondage,
the squat tortoise at noon, the gangling hank
at sunset. We have parodied the body

of the dog, the cat, the horse, but never hatched
so many creatures fashioned without hands.

Colloquy

A handyman, is it, now? And what can hands
do more than minds about it? Pull the curtains?
Fidget with pens? Settle a tinker's haggle?

– Your hand, man, from the grave, and in my cursive
so studiously unlike yours, old bible ham;
give me your hand, conclude this running skirmish.

Give me your hand; you never gave me a hand.

– The dead can't plead for those that live and suffer;
the living may not pray for the dead. The has been

is forever has been. Advise your son
while he is still alive. Put him wise.
Feed experience to his wide presumption!

Trust you to put it straight in black and white.

– Or the old block will know the reason why.

He Addresses Himself to Reflection

The minnow leaves have made no headway yet.
The only way is down, for all their darting,
and they, like you, go down without a yelp.

Father, father, no more; the glass is dark.
I've put the light out. Now the moths have gone.
You've never haunted darkness, poor cadaver.

You're laid to rest. I give my word as gospel.
I suppose I'll watch the leaves, the squirrel
a few more years, still heckle autumn's gossip,

sometimes catch your tones. I cannot acquit you.
And this abeyance gives no satisfaction.
Lie easy as ever – and forgive this quibble.

– Years, years spent pouring words we couldn't fathom.
Only through death we speak in honest fashion.

Ventriloquy

My son, you haunt me with my hasty youth.
The genes have won! And nothing I have tried
has saved you from the worst, or been much use.

You look at me as I have stared in triumph
over my father, seeing only what seemed
incomprehension, suffering his casual triteness.

I don't much like the glare of your conceit.
I've lived your mood. You haven't reached my mood
or feeling, history or hope, season for season.

If you look, there is a blue tinge to the moon.
Sliver of apple on the knife. – My voyage
is almost over; your promontory is moving.

Who's speaking, please? Father, is this your voice?
Late, so late. The line is dead. Void, void.

* * *

NEW POEMS

A Time to Speak

I wanted to say much more than this.
But at the time with all the talk
I couldn't think how best to speak.

The time of our life in front of us,
but I misjudged how long it took
weighing the moment I should pick.

You'd turn, I thought, towards me, torn
to utter that long-building cry
half gathered through your idioms.

I've been too quiet. You didn't turn,
but like a wild bird wintering came
to me ... and I have given you crumbs.

– Is it a bearable snow? Don't leave.
Don't go.... This waiting has been love.

Outcry

The pain is within me, wordless.
Why should I cry out
and add it to the world's?

You neither, don't you speak,
and for the same reason.
Don't try a single scream.

If my hand were in your hair
we could short-circuit the world.
What a stroke that would be!

Platonic

You never raped my soul – and that is why
I hate you. Everything you thought you'd had:
my little finger, lips, my barefoot pad,
tilt of the head, fishnet across a thigh,
as if these held in truth the very thing.
And the old burrow to the familiar dark,
your knick-knack cyclotron to hold that spark
in vacuo by conjuring in the ring!

Your soul, poor stump, has never made my soul.
But mine would soon have shown you what rape is,
if you were of my kind, near my black hole.
– Dream easier to chase, death easier to lay,
than going round this corner where I turn away.
This birch I touch into your memories.

Parting Gift

This is my last and lasting gift to you:
a locket. Empty, and empty will remain.
I bind you here with all the force I can raise:
give it the next hapless, willowy goof
to shack up with you.
                          – This you'll never do.
First, it's too complicated to explain;
best, your last chance to cross me all your days.
Go on. Right now. Fling it over the roof.

Not something to remember till you die,
my planted bug. You'll not forget: you ditch
the damn thing, hide, or give it. She's to try
to keep or junk it. You'll remember this bitch.
A locket. Empty. A singularity,
black voidlet that will waste you. Only me!

World Tour

Wherever you shall go, whatever do,
I shall be there. Just wait. Shut all the doors.
Yes, yes. I know it physically can't be true.
And mind, I'd never hang about in yours.
And as for metaphor, I've lost you there.
And you would think I'd have at least to die,
to die and, desiccated into air,
blow all about the world to catch your eye.

But you forget the language! Try foreign parts!
I'll mark some words with me, my direct line,
dearest, till death ... you lie with. I'll spring on you
like guilt from words you seldom used or knew,
forgive me. And daily shock you with your arts
and crafts, your sniping hatreds. Vengeance is mine ...

Journey

Dearest, I've gone at your pace.
We've lingered on the way;
some route you chose to trace!
It's taken us all day.

Let's have some give and take.
You've named the flowers. Look sharp.
It's not so far to make.
I'm going down that scarp.

That way we're there by dark.
Ah no, don't name the stars!
Sidereal meadow-spark?
Well, not all the stars.

Autumn Colour

How you laugh each year to watch the sparrows
flying in, and almost hidden, filching
berries from the firethorn. You can spare them.

That low laugh is why I like their fling,
wondering how the little buggers miss
impalement on the barbs a good inch long.

Some of them have stripped the elder tree.
You'd planted that for two good sorts of wine.
We wonder which prefer it or if all try.

How many other women used to love
watching through time these sparrows dart and hide
to steal their better thoughts and give a laugh!

You planted it for autumn colour once,
now for the birds in winter – part of our life.
And that low laugh, one of my seasonal wants.

You'd have planted it for all those women,
if you had ever known them, anticipating
your life and mine.
                    The birds are almost human,

shaking their beaks like fingers stuck to paper.

Monologue

Years? It seems an aeon
that I have kept faith,
whatever that might mean
without volition or oath.
You left me little option –
Your talents, your serial spleens!
Always the exception,
you with your fine lines.

But I know what it means
in slither, self-disgust,
and icy blue moons.
Not that you'd have guessed.
Fat chance you're flesh and blood
The last far pane of light
has flicked down like a lid.
The night is absolute.

– But isn't there some plane,
abstract, where the stars arch,
or at least Himalayan,
where this would count for much,
some brilliant white space?
And might this plane be yours?
Where we'd come to the odd pass
to tally the dead years?

– I cannot stop the mind
throwing you up again,
in its world without end,
neither has been nor bygone.
Shall we ever break even?
How tortured in my mind
your twists and turns are woven.
This hell I recommend.

Bequest

Your rear-view mirror onto happiness –
you used to call it that if ever asked:
the scene is anywhere, too picturesque.
A stream meanders, glinting; two paths
meet at a bridge symmetrically, repeat
odd patterns from the winding of the stream.

A keepsake of you? You knew there was no need.
How could a meagre bit of earth dismiss
what years and miles had never done? The scene,
the long cherishing, is your farewell gift.
As you'd have wished, it hangs now on my wall –
the distance fringed with pines where I would walk.

But what you saw and treasured on that bridge,
or who you met there then – or down which path? –
and where you stood to want this view of it
I cannot bring to mind on your behalf.
What you have cherished here I can't possess.
The two paths merge your absence into death.

NOTES

THE STORMS

Dedication
In the original edition, there was no forename and the acrostic was not highlighted in any way. My editor at that time, Kevin Crossley-Holland, the translator of *Beowulf*, with his skill in Saxon metrics, is, so far as I know, the only one who noticed the dodge.

Meditation Down the Wards
This poem is the earliest I have selected, the first that ever made me feel I could write. It records the shock of coming straight from a cosy grammar school and an evangelical Christian background to work as a porter in a hospital. The following four poems reflect the same experience, as does 'Radium Therapy', first published in *Mortal Fire* (see p. 41).

Obtainable from All Good Herbalists'
This herbalist, in New Inn Hall Street, Oxford, was well-known for selling condoms, too. An undergraduate I knew remarked of the proprietor: 'He's like a father-confessor.'

MORTAL FIRE

The Fragments
'Unaddressed Letter' and this poem are the only two poems in this selection where I have made changes rather to the matter than to the form of the text, and for very complicated reasons. In my late forties I returned – in 'Mirrors, Windows' – to the father-son theme. In the course of this sequence I remarked: 'Give me your hand, conclude this running skirmish.' I know art is not action, that poetry 'makes nothing happen', but I am caught here in a double bind. It would be in some way dishonest to have said that line without at least some curtailing of the skirmish in these early poems. Hindsight suggests that the difficulties of the father-son relationship are more general than personal.

The quotation at the head of the poem is from a book of hymns by Albert Orsborn: *The Secret of his Presence*. The author became the General of the Salvation Army during my childhood. It was a teenage sense of irony that found an inn-sign in the quotation.

Full Circle
The book is *Moonfleet* by J. Meade Falkner. The obscure remark about seniors in verse 3 refers to an evil practice in the school where I then taught which consisted in distributing classes of absent teachers among the classes of teachers who had space – irrespective of subject or year-level.

ONE ANOTHER
I have removed three sonnets from the original sequence since they introduced new characters too late in the narrative and led to confusion. This change has led to a slight alteration in 'Record' earlier in the series. I have also added a sonnet 'The Game' which arrived too late for inclusion originally but which should now clarify events a little.

Bird's Eye
'Birsy' in the last line is the imagined future corruption of 'bird's eye' on analogy with 'daisy/day's eye'.

TOO MUCH OF WATER

Byway
This poem has a curious rhyme-scheme. I was looking for something effective but unobtrusive to mark line-ends and came up with an identical vowel-sound on the light syllable before the final stress. I thought it unobtrusive but a student in a workshop noticed it instantly.

Clusters
The emotion in this sonnet is dependent on the idea that the universe is so vast that the earth and all that is on it must repeat somewhere in time and space. Some developments in quantum theory also suggest this repeatability.

Against Superstition
The occasion for the writing of this poem was a request to provide something for an issue of a magazine celebrating the work of Donald Davie. Curiously, though holding to the decision stated in the first verse, the following three poems rapidly turned up. (The decision did not refer to poems dedicating volumes, which are a traditional and special case, but was caused by the plentiful name-dropping matiness of much verse.)

An Apology
The circumstances surrounding this poem are entirely literary, I am afraid. I had been fairly critical of Lowell's *Notebook* (1970), closely followed by its rewrite *History* (1973), when I was given the chance to improve my own *Mortal Fire* of 1970. I felt I could not do so without some sort of apology to Lowell. And, after all, if earlier versions of books can be discounted, what could be fairer than discarding old reviews? Oddly, it was an exchange of letters with Lowell, and a consideration of his fourteen-line rhymeless sonnet-form used in both volumes that led me to the sonnets of *One Another*.

EARTH LIGHT

Willow Walk
The word 'forehead', v. 2, rhymes with 'horrid'.

LIKE A VOW
I am indebted to the following friends who read the sequence and made valuable suggestions: Humphrey Clucas, Kevin Crossley-Holland, Kenneth Crowhurst and Roland John.

The Sunken Path
v. 8, l.12. I pronounce the word 'lichen' as 'liken'.

A Woman Speaks to God the Father
This poem turned up verbatim in a dream. The only waking change I had to make was to replace 'perpetual' with 'endless' in the last line for rhythmical purposes.

MIRRORS, WINDOWS

The Garden Beyond and Beyond
l. 7. Just after the Second World War, fountain-pens were expensive objects not lightly given to children. Torches were magical toys also, after all those years of eking every last glimmer out of more or less flat batteries.

INDEX OF TITLES

A Likeness Reflects, 148
A Little Light, 77
A Long Shot, 87
A Time to Speak, 157
A Woman Speaks to God the Father, 145
Against Superstition, 114
An Apology, 115
Antique, 124
Aubade, 81
Autumn Colour, 160
Autumnal, 99
Bats, 33
Before Sleep, 100
Bequest, 162
Bird's Eye, 89
Birds, 115
Bric-a-Brac, 126
Byway, 108
Clear Stream, 97
Clearing, 101
Clusters, 110
Colloquy, 152
Comfort, 92
Communication, 143
Compact, 91
Cone, 76
Correspondences, 142
Country Walk, 53
Courtesy Visit, 43
Cranesbill, 121
Crocus, 56
Crowd, 50
Damages, 47
Deadlock, 62
Declination, 80
Dedication (*The Storms*), 18
Dedication (*Mortal Fire*), 36
Dedication (*Too Much of Water*), 111
Deed of Gift, 84
Dialogue and Soliloquy, 76
Dissolve, 75
Dream, 91
Duotone, 96
Dusk (*One Another*), 98
Dusk (THE GOING), 55
Earth-bound, 104
Eidetic Image, 65
Eighth Period, 21
Exorcism, 113
Fledgling, 93
Frost, 86
Full Circle, 48
Gesture, 135
Gift of Words, 55
Gifts (*One Another*), 113
Gifts (*Earth Light*), 122
Gifts (THE GOING), 59
Glimpses, 94
Goldenrod, 125
Hand and Head, 86
HAVING NO ALTERNATIVE, 45
He Addresses Himself to Reflection, 153
Hearing the Flowers, 95
Her Concentration on a Nutshell, 83
Her Prophecy, 94
Hold, 57
Homage to Robinson Jeffers, 146
Impasse, 62
Inklings, 93
Insight, 63
Insights, 78

Interflora, 108
Journey, 159
Just Visiting, 28
Keeper, 60
Keepsake, 63
Landscape, 74
Last Respects, 25
Last Wishes, 107
Last Words, 107
Life-Lines, 144
LIKE A VOW, 128
Local Colour, 128
Long Evenings, 102
Lost and Found, 58
Lullaby (*Mortal Fire*), 45
Lullaby (THE GOING), 57
Match, 79
Meander, 60
Meditation Down the Wards, 25
Meeting, 42
Memento (*Earth Light*), 123
Memento (*One Another*), 90
Memorial (*Earth Light*), 147
Memorial (*One Another*), 103
Mirrors, 127
MIRRORS, WINDOWS, 148
Moment, 110
Monologue, 161
THE MONTHS, 30
Moon, 85
Moth, 102
Moth-Light, 98
Music, 82
Not Drinking Water, 24
Obsession, 65
Obtainable from All Good
 Herbalists', 29
Occasions, 122
Old Haunt, 58
Old Poet on a Rainy Day, 51

ONE ANOTHER, 73
One Another, 90
One Off, 103
Outcry, 157
Overnight Coach, 21
Parting Gift, 158
Passing the Gates, 26
Path, 112
Patient in a Ward, 26
Platonic, 158
Portents, 121
Presence, 54
Present, 92
Pressed, 83
Radium Therapy, 41
Rain, 71
Recapitulation, 128
Recognition, 71
Record, 87
Reflection Answers Back, 149
Reflection Heckles, 152
Reflection Rebukes and
 Challenges, 150
Rendezvous, 109
Response, 75
Retraction, 62
Retrospect, 60
Returns, 55
Revenant, 101
River, 138
River-Garden, 31
Separation, 46
Shades, 85
Shadow, 81
Silence, 80
Silver Birch, 54
Single Ticket, 23
Sleep, 57
Souvenir, 143
Spectrum, 97

Spring, 108
Starting Your Travels, 47
Steps (*Mortal Fire*), 46
Steps (*Earth Light*), 145
Still, 141
Storm, 88
Summer Shadows, 116
Sun, 142
Sunset and Storm, 84
Talisman, 79
Tangibles, 52
Terrace, 50
The Brooch, 111
The Fragments, 38
The Game, 99
The Garden Beyond, 148
The Garden Beyond and Beyond, 150
THE GOING, 52
The Hill, 137
The Lane, 74
The Lost Ones, 144
The Mind's Eye, 64
The Oak, 100
The Rose, 77
The Shadow, 87
The Storms, 19
The Sunken Path, 133
The Swifts, 53
The Terms, 43
The Thunder Stone, 88
The Visitors, 27
The Water-Splash, 140
Thinking of Writing a Letter, 44
Thirty Summers, 50
Thrush, 31
Tie, 61
Truce, 61
Twilight, 61
Two Sparrows, 59
Unaddressed Letter, 37
Unspoken, 72
Upland, 130
Ventriloquy, 154
View, 82
Vigil, 66
Violets, 124
Wait and See, 52
Walk from the House, 37
Walk, 89
Wall, 112
Wild Flower, 66
Willow Walk, 123
Window, 104
Winter, 30
Winters, 114
Wise and Cautious, 151
Word, 109
World Tour, 159

Dante
THE DIVINE COMEDY
HELL · PURGATORY · HEAVEN

in a terza rima translation by
PETER DALE

Dante's masterpiece is a foundation stone of European poetry. It was a profound influence on T. S. Eliot and Ezra Pound, and in our own day has inspired Seamus Heaney. It is simple in style yet complex in its layers of meaning, episodic in manner yet architectonic in its over-arching vision. It is simultaneously a journey through life and a spiritual biography, a portrait of the internecine Italy of Dante's time and a Pilgrim's Progress through the tripartite afterworld of Catholic mythology. Paradoxically, it is also a devotional work and one of the strangest love poems ever written. It is without doubt one of the supreme works of world literature.

Peter Dale has already established a reputation as one of this country's leading translators for his *François Villon: Selected Poems*, and more recently for his witty and accurate versions of Jules Laforgue. His great achievement here has been to produce a version of *The Divine Comedy* in modern English that echoes Dante's 'sweet new style' while keeping to the poet's demanding *terza rima* verse pattern. It is a reader's edition – accurate, clear and compelling. It is also Peter Dale's crowning achievement as a translator.

POEMS OF JULES LAFORGUE

Translated from the French by
PETER DALE

'He is an exquisite poet, a deliverer of nations ... a father of light', said Ezra Pound in 1918 of Jules Laforgue, the iconoclastic manipulator of the French language who died in Paris at the age of twenty-seven. Like Poe, Laforgue has been a more influential poet abroad than at home. His innovatory handling of free verse, for example, was an inspiration to the young T. S. Eliot, who was also drawn to his tone of urban wit and the way his poetry, part-symbolist and part-impressionist, reflected the uncertainties of modern city life. Laforgue's associative method, speech-rhythms, his new and daring rhymes, boldly heterogeneous diction and his untrammelled imagination make him one of the quirkiest, most individual and entertaining of French poets, who was also notable for his early protests for the liberation of women.

Peter Dale captures the resourceful energy and panache of Laforgue's poetry in translations which are by turns as playful, wild, clear, obscure and impossible as the French poems.

'Laforgue is so much more vigorous than English Laforguianism ... when Dale adapts, he still manages to reproduce, conveying much of the letter of the original as well as the spirit ... The collection is hard to overpraise'

D. J. ENRIGHT, *Observer*

New and Recent Poetry from Anvil

HEATHER BUCK
Psyche Unbound

TONY CONNOR
Metamorphic Adventures

DICK DAVIS
Touchwood

DICK DAVIS
Borrowed Ware
MEDIEVAL PERSIAN EPIGRAMS

MICHAEL HAMBURGER
Collected Poems 1941–1994

JAMES HARPUR
The Monk's Dream

ANTHONY HOWELL
First Time in Japan

IVAN V. LALIĆ
A Rusty Needle
TRANSLATED BY FRANCIS R. JONES

THOMAS McCARTHY
The Lost Province

E. A. MARKHAM
Misapprehensions

PETER RUSSELL
The Elegies of Quintilius

RUTH SILCOCK
A Wonderful View of the Sea

A catalogue of our publications is available on request